DATE DUE			
FEB 12 '8			
DEC 16 '83'S			
NOV 10 '84'S			
JAN 17 '85'S			
OCT 29 '85'S			
OCT 29 '86'S			
NOV 4'87'S			
OCT 31 '90'S			
JUL 13 '91'S			

BONDS

How To Double Your Money Quickly & Safely

BONDS

How To Double Your Money Quickly & Safely

by

Robert Lawrence Holt

California Financial Publications
1980

Library of Congress Cataloging in Publication Data

Holt, Robert Lawrence

BONDS: How To Double Your Money Quickly & Safely

Includes index.
1. Bonds—Securities—Interest. I. Title.
HG4651.H65   1980   332.6'32   80-66576
ISBN 0-930926-03-X

CALIFORNIA FINANCIAL PUBLICATIONS
3900 Shenandoah Drive
Oceanside, CA 92054

First Edition

1   2   3   4   5   6   7   8   9   10

....dedicated to my parents,
who instilled in me a strong
sense of the value of capital.

PREFACE

For the majority of persons who wish to know more about bonds, there is nowhere to turn. Most stockbrokers know little concerning this subject. Local newspapers and newscasts rarely comment on the bond market. The "Wall Street Journal" has a daily column on bonds which is primarily concerned with a few new issues, a limited coverage considering that there are more than 5700 bonds listed in the monthly "Bond Guide." New "Bond Guides" are almost impossible to obtain from brokerages.

Bonds seem to be one of Wall Street's best kept secrets, yet they are one of the safest methods of substantially increasing one's income or capital---goals of almost everyone.

I first entered the securities industry in 1961 and quickly learned that long-term success was wholly dependent on the well-being and growth of my clientele's capital. My background spanned all areas of the brokerage business. I was offered managership of a commodities department, later served as an options coordinator, and eventually was appointed as the manager of institutional accounts at the Los Angeles branch of one of the largest firms on Wall Street. Specialization in the field of bond securities was responsible for my being the most senior account executive of this firm in southern California at the age of 32.

This book, the first in its field to be written by a professional experienced in working with the public, provides the guidelines which enabled my customers to maximize their income and capital. Having taught thousands of investors at securities seminars during the past two decades, I know the questions bond investors ask. This book answers them.

R.L.H.

CONTENTS

THE BOND MARKET

FINDING THE RIGHT BONDS FOR YOUR NEEDS

ESTABLISHING YOUR BOND PROGRAM

Chapter 1

Should You Own Bonds?

Although information concerning bond investments is seldom discussed in commonly-read or viewed media, bonds have existed for many hundreds of years. The total volume of bonds outstanding in the United States now exceeds $1.5 trillion. Of this amount, about $748 billion has been issued by the U.S. Treasury and other federal agencies, $313 billion by local and state governments, and $455 billion by corporations. During the 1970s the volume of bonds almost tripled from $575 billion, encouraging a wider interest among all investors.

Due to the generous yields offered during the 1970s, individual investors were purchasing as much as $30 billion annually, about 6 times the previous volume. Although future bond yields will generally fluctuate with the business cycle, attractive yields should continue to be available with reasonable frequency.

*

WHAT IS A BOND?

A bond is an interest-bearing certificate issued by a business corporation or a government agency. It promises to pay the holder specific interest payments on particular dates, usually every 6 months. Most bonds are initially issued at their par value ($1000), and at the bond's maturity date the issuer is obligated to redeem the bond at par value.

One of the most widely-held bond issues is the American Telephone and Telegraph 8.8% 2005 debenture. Each of these bonds pays $88 interest per year, in the form of semi-annual payments of $44 on May 15 and November 15. AT&T is obligated to redeem these bonds at $1000 on May 15, 2005; although they may be redeemed earlier under certain conditions. This bond trades every business day on the New York Stock Exchange, as bond investors buy and sell according to their financial needs.

There are two major reasons for owning bonds:

1. to increase your income, and
2. to increase your capital.

As a vehicle for these goals, bonds can offer both safety and a reasonable rate of return.

*

ARE YOU READY FOR BONDS?

Prior to purchasing bonds, it is important to examine one's needs. Such examination may reveal that several personal needs should receive attention before bonds are considered.

☐ Do You Have An Adequate Home?

The cost of owning a home has been increasing rapidly in recent years, and the cost of renting has increased almost as fast. When funds are available, every family should consider home ownership. The benefits are many. In the first place, it is necessary to pay for living space whether renting or owning. Usually for 25% to 35% higher monthly costs, a family can own their home instead of renting. At the end of each tax year, most of these higher costs will be balanced by tax benefits (deductions of both interest and taxes).

In the long run, the most important benefit of home ownership is protection from inflation. Home ownership usually assures that a family will be able to own a home regardless of the rate of inflation. Families who continue to rent through periods of high inflation may find themselves priced out of their preferred living areas when they wish to change rental locations.

When a family does not have sufficient funds for a downpayment on a home, they may find bonds useful in the accumulation of such capital. How this can be accomplished is discussed thoroughly in the following chapters, particularly Chapter 6.

☐ Is Your Family Protected by Insurance?

In all families, the life of the wage-earner(s) should be adequately protected by both life and health insurance. Many families realize that much more life insurance for the same premium can be obtained by purchasing *term* insurance instead of whole-life insurance. Whole-life insurance costs considerably more as the insured person has the option of surrendering their policy for a "savings value," which is usually very minimal compared to other savings investments. Term insurance normally has no surrender value.

When purchasing term insurance, it is also wise to add "double indemnity" to the policy. This doubles the insured amount in case of accidental death — the most probable cause among young heads of households.

If a family's questions are not clearly and intelligently answered by a particular insurance agent, it may not be the

11

fault of the questions. As insurance agents essentially are salespersons who must rely on commissions for their income, it may be wise to seek presentations from other agents when satisfactory answers are not provided.

Mãny times a family will be surprised by the wide difference in premiums among insurance companies for the same coverage. Shop around before making a final choice. Those who do not consider all alternatives often pay far too much for their insurance needs.

☐ Are Other Security Investments "Insecure?"

Many persons may have already tried to make money with their capital in the stock market, the options market, the commodities exchanges, and other high-risk areas. The frustration experienced by such investors is usually matched by the size of their losses. Only specialists in these fields have a chance to break-even or make money in the long run. Most others pay these specialists for the privilege of venturing into unfamiliar territory.

Many investors hope for immediate capital gains when purchasing common stocks. When these purchases do not yield such short-term results, their owners then begin to call the holdings "long-term" investments. Although this bit of rationalization may ease the mind, it does little for the capital.

The new investor in bonds will find that the level of *emotional involvement* is much less in comparison to speculating in other securities. Whereas emotional factors often dominate the decisions of speculators, the investor in bonds has little cause to make decisions which are not carefully weighed.

☐Are The Burdens Of Property Management Unacceptable?

In periods of rapid (double-digit) inflation, the ownership of attractive real estate can be quite rewarding. However, many persons find that the purchase and management of real estate offers more problems than rewards.

As with any investment, it is important to purchase property at the proper price level. If the buyer mistakenly pays too high a price, it may be difficult if not impossible to make the property pay for itself. Rental income might turn out to be substantially less than the actual cost of carrying the property. In moderately difficult times, owners of such real estate may find it necessary to periodically place additional capital into their holdings in order to meet mortgage, tax, maintenance, and other costs. The alternative can be the loss of the property, which may include the loss of one's capital also.

The most common complaint of rental property owners is perhaps the aggravation of continual maintenance requirements and the handling of their tenants. When a plumbing or heating problem arises, tenants expect instant attention regardless of the day or hour. Unruly, slow-paying, or non-paying tenants may pose worse problems.

For the above reasons, many real estate specialists recommend the purchase of rental property only if its size is sufficient to allow professional management.

☐ Is Personal Property Oriented Toward Appreciation?

Many families have found that a $500 antique sofa offers more long-term comfort (both human and financial) than a new sofa. Antique items can be used to attractively decorate a home and are excellent hedges against inflation.

Even automobiles can offer some protection against inflation. Recent models of luxury cars (Eldorado Cadillacs and Rivieras), moderately-priced cars (pre-1974 Mustangs), sports cars (early Thunderbirds and Jaguars), and all convertibles can provide drivers both transportation and modest yearly appreciation. The cost of acquiring most of these "classics" is quite reasonable compared to the price of many new cars.

The purchase of rare stamps, coins, antique dishware, silverware, jewelry, books, paintings and sketches, and other "collectibles" can also be good investments which provide personal enjoyment. The reader is cautioned to avoid most advertised sources for such collectibles, as the buyer may be paying as much for the advertising as they are for value in the product. If some of the "unbelievably" high returns were as easily obtained, they would certainly not require such heavy advertising.

☐ Protect Your Capital First

If you work for the capital you accumulate, the first consideration before any investment should be the *protection of the capital*. It can be very difficult to replace lost capital.

13

Most investors find that the safest investments are those which have good liquidity. These investments permit the withdrawal of capital at any time, without delay. The reader will find that bonds offer a comparatively high degree of liquidity, which may explain why the vast majority of bonds are now held by corporations, pension and profit-sharing trusts, banks, and other large institutions.

*

WHERE ARE YOUR SAVINGS NOW?

In the United States, many persons customarily place their excess funds into savings accounts at local banks and thrift institutions, in whole-life insurance policies, or in U.S. savings bonds.

With the exception of the U.S. government, these organizations must manage their affairs in a manner which covers their expenses. Consequently, they seek a higher rate of interest on their deposits than they pay to their public depositors, sometimes substantially higher.

The federal government tightly controls maximum interest levels which banks and savings institutions can pay their depositors. These controls encourage the meager yields the institutions pay to the public. Present regulations permit a maximum interest rate on ordinary savings (passbook) accounts of 5¼% at banks and 5½% at savings and loan institutions.

On June 22, 1979, U.S. Treasury Secretary W. Michael Blumenthal told Congress:

> "Current laws and regulations actually penalize those wishing to save. Between 1968 and 1979, federal limits on savings account interest cost Americans $42 billion in lost earnings, and $19 billion of that burden was carried by persons over the age of 65."

☐ Bank Savings Accounts

Banks, of course, loan some of the public's deposits to other members of the public. They also invest these deposits in vast quantities of corporate and municipal bonds. During the early months of 1979, banks and insurance companies actually purchased sufficient amounts of tax-free municipal bonds to account for the entire new supply of such bonds (several billion dollars worth.)

While banks were paying individual depositors a taxable 5% interest rate during early 1979 on ordinary savings accounts, the same banks were transferring these savings into corporate bonds paying more than 9% and into tax-free municipal bonds paying from 6% to 7%.

An individual in a 25% tax bracket with funds in a 5% bank savings account earns an after-tax yield of 3.75% (the difference between 5% and 1.25%). If these funds were invested instead in the same tax-free bonds as the banks were purchasing in early 1979, this individual could have earned an after-tax yield of 7% — almost a doubling of one's income. A substantial income increase could have been obtained by purchasing taxable corporate bonds also.

The fact that many persons give up this additional income to their banking institutions is partially reflected in the profitability of the general banking industry. Recent earnings records of a few of the largest U. S. banks are:

BANK	(Earnings Per Share)			
	1976	1977	1978	1979
Bank of America	$2.40	$2.71	$3.53	$4.10
Chase Manhattan	3.28	3.71	5.59	9.07
Mellon National	3.31	3.62	4.40	5.17

☐ Savings And Loan Accounts

How the public's funds are re-invested by thrift institutions is well-known by anyone who has a home loan. For many years now home loan rates have exceeded 9%, frequently ranging much higher. During this same time period, savings and loan institutions have paid the public only 5¼% to 5½% on ordinary savings accounts.

Of course, higher yields than those are available in long-term certificate accounts at savings and loan institutions; however, there are *five serious drawbacks* to these accounts:

1. if savings must be withdrawn before maturity, there are severe penalties (loss of 3 month's interest for certificates of one year or less, or loss of 6 month's interest for certificates maturing in more than one year),
2. if general interest rates increase, one's savings are already tied up and these higher rates cannot be taken advantage of without premature withdrawal penalties,
3. if general interest rates decline substantially, new savings and loan certificate rates may be considerably lower when current certificates mature,
4. if general interest rates have declined over a lengthy period of time, savings and loan institutions may restrict the amount that depositors can place in certificates (they have in the past) or the availability of new certificates may be completely eliminated, and
5. when general interest rates decline appreciably, premature withdrawal penalties may discourage depositors from participating in capital gains available in the bond market.

With such wide disparities between what savings and loan institutions generally pay the public for savings deposits and the high yields at which these funds are then re-invested, it is little wonder that many of these corporations have doubled their profits during the last few years:

SAVINGS & LOAN	(Earnings Per Share)			
	1976	1977	1978	1979
Biscayne Fed S & L	$1.54	$2.29	$2.81	$3.23
Far West Financial	1.41	2.41	3.47	4.10
Financial Corp. Amer.	0.91	1.60	2.21	3.13

Certainly, there is justification for families to retain small amounts of emergency funds in accounts at savings and loan institutions. However, we will learn that larger sums can be placed where they will yield far more for most persons.

☐ Whole-Life Insurance Policies

We learned earlier that insurance companies are among the largest buyers of tax-free municipal bonds. They also purchase vast amounts of taxable corporate bonds. The relatively-large premiums which individuals pay when they buy whole-life insurance policies (the most commonly-held) are used to purchase these bonds.

Insurance agents encourage their customers to think of whole-life insurance as a "form of savings." According to the Federal Trade Commission, the average yield of such savings is *1.3%*. Michael Pertschuk, chairman of the Federal Trade Commission, aptly describes whole-life insurance in the following words:

> "No other product in our economy that is purchased by so many people for so much money is bought with so little understanding of its actual or comparative value."

A 1979 Federal Trade Commission report reveals that consumers annually spend $30 billion on whole-life insurance premiums. As in the case of large banks and the savings and loan industry, most life insurance companies operate quite profitably:

INSURANCE COMPANY	(Earnings Per Share)			
	1976	1977	1978	1979
Aetna Life	$2.61	5.17	6.39	6.93
Amer. Heritage Life	1.25	1.38	1.51	1.80
Farmers Group	1.60	2.08	2.50	3.00

At the end of 1978, Federal Reserve data revealed that assets of life insurance companies totaled $378 billion.

□ U. S. Savings Bonds

As educational levels improve, fewer persons are placing or leaving their savings in U.S. savings bonds. On May 11, 1979 a government spokeswoman reported that redemptions of these bonds had exceeded purchases since July of 1978. Perhaps this is why the government increased the interest rate on these bonds from 6% to 6½% in May of 1979. On January 1, 1980 this rate was increased again to 7%, providing an owner holds their bonds for a minimum of 11 years.

Few persons realize that if series "E" U.S. savings bonds are redeemed within 6 months of their purchase, all accumulated interest is *forfeited*. If such bonds are redeemed after two years, the holder receives *only 4%* on their savings instead of the advertised 7%. It is only by keeping these bonds for the long-term that the stated return is obtained.

Certain "patriotic" Americans exhort the public to purchase these bonds periodically in the media. During peacetime there is little justification to purchase these bonds. Investing in low-yield U.S. savings bonds might be considered a form of public *subsidy* for government spending. It is unfortunate that the Americans who purchase these bonds are generally those with lower educational and income levels who can least afford to be sacrificing their savings income.

☐ Why Sacrifice Income To The Middleman?

Continual advertising messages encourage us to place our savings in low-yielding accounts with banks, savings and loans, and other thrift institutions. These "middleman" institutions are anxious to receive our savings, as we have seen that they can usually re-invest such funds at a substantial profit.

There is little reason why individuals should permit these middlemen to re-invest their savings; however, persons who would never consider paying a 50% commission to sell their homes often sacrifice half of their potential savings income to these middlemen. We will learn that any individual can purchase essentially the same high-yielding taxable or tax-free bonds that these institutions so profitably purchase.

*

HOW CAN BONDS HELP FIGHT INFLATION?

During periods of inflation, there are numerous methods of improving one's income or capital with bonds. Of course, *when and how* such bonds are purchased is just as important as which ones are chosen.

☐ Purchasing Discount Bonds

Discount bonds are previously-issued bonds which are selling below par ($1000). The most common reason for a bond to be selling at a discount is because general interest rates have increased over the rate prevailing when the bond was first issued.

Due to their *fixed* rate of interest, bonds fluctuate in price to remain attractive to new buyers. As general interest rates increase, bond prices decline proportionally; and conversely, lower interest rates levels lead to higher bond prices.

The astute bond buyer should observe interest rate trends for periods when rates are peaking. When these rates appear to have reached their highest levels, intelligent purchases of discount bonds can lead to substantial capital gains in ensuing years. When a discount bond increases in price during a period of falling interest rates, a new owner derives two benefits:

1. the developing capital gain, and
2. a superior current yield.

For example, let us assume that in the current year the average newly-issued bond has a 10% yield (coupon rate); while 3 years earlier new bonds were issued with 9% coupons. The price of the 3-year-old 9% bonds probably will have declined in value to approximately $900 to reflect currently-available yields. At a price of $900, the 9% bonds would offer *new buyers* a 10% current yield ($90 coupon divided by price of $900).

New buyers have a choice, either of purchasing a new-issue 10% bond at $1000 *or* a 3-year-old 9% bond at $900. The buyer who is interested in both income and capital gains would choose the discounted 9% bond. As interest rate levels fluctuate during following years, a return to a 9% general interest rate level would cause the 9% bond to increase in value back to $1000; hence the buyers of this bond will have a $100 capital gain in addition to earning their 10% current yield. On a yearly basis, overall returns of twenty per cent (or more) are possible when discount bonds have been carefully chosen during periods of high interest rates.

The buyer of the 10% coupon bond which was a new-issue will also have a capital gain, although it will not be as large due to the possibility of redemption at par (discussed in the following chapter).

□ Sheltering Capital In Custodial Accounts

Families with children should consider placing a portion of excess funds in custodial bond accounts for their children. This transfers income and capital gains from the parent's tax bracket to the child's lower tax bracket. The establishment of a custodial account is an excellent method of quickly building a college education fund.

☐ Sheltering Capital In Retirement Accounts

Employees who are not covered by retirement plans at their place of employment can establish "Individual Retirement Arrangements (IRAs). Yearly contributions to an IRA account are limited to 15% of one's income, up to a maximum of either $1500 or $1750 depending on one's marital status. Such contributions are *tax-deductible;* and in addition, resulting income and capital gains *are not taxed* until years later when one retires.

Self-employed persons can contribute much more to "defined contribution" retirement plans called Keogh accounts. Their contributions also are limited to 15% of their income, however the maximum amount is $7500. Tax benefits are similar to those of an IRA account.

Certain self-employed individuals with exceptionally high incomes (over the 50% tax bracket) may find it advantageous to use a "defined benefit" form of a Keogh account. This type of plan often permits contributions which are *double* the normal limits allowed for Keogh accounts.

Whichever form of retirement account is utilized, the *source* of contributions does not necessarily have to be from one's income. Funds for these contributions can come from the sale of common stock investments, savings accounts, or any other source of cash. One's yearly income figure is only used to calculate the *allowable percentage* of such contributions.

The establishment of these retirement accounts is the most rapid method of *doubling one's capital.* At interest rates which have prevailed in recent years (10% to 15%), the doubling of one's initial investment has been possible *within 5 to 7 years.* These funds would triple within another 3 to 4 years.

IRA and defined contribution Keogh accounts can be quickly opened at most brokerages. Establishment of a defined *benefit* plan requires prior approval of an actuary (insurance specialist) who is qualified to practice before the Internal Revenue Service. How to set up these accounts is thoroughly discussed in Chapter 15.

☐ Convertible Bonds And Capital Gains

In addition to interest, convertible bonds offer the holder an option of converting to a specified number of common shares of the same corporation. When the common stock appreciates above a particular price, the bond begins to fluctuate at an equal pace.

Opportunities for capital gains are limited by the intelligence and experience of the bond buyer *and* the fickleness of the stock market. In some stock markets, virtually no one makes capital gains in convertible bonds. And even in the best of stock markets, it's necessary for the investor to purchase the "right" bonds in order to obtain capital gains. Realistic approaches to convertible bond investments are discussed in Chapter 5.

*

FORMING A SUCCESSFUL BOND PROGRAM

Experienced persons know that success in most endeavors involves careful investigation and planning.

☐ Setting Your Goals: Income Or Capital Gains

The first step for the prospective bond buyer is to decide which is the most important goal:

1. more income, or
2. capital gains.

Many individuals, especially retired persons, are primarily interested in increasing their current *spendable* income. Having this goal, it is necessary to seek out those bonds with high yields which are not likely to be redeemed in the near future. When one's tax bracket is over 30%, it also may be wise to review tax-free yields available in municipal bonds.

Persons whose primary goal is capital gains must first determine which, if any, *retirement plans* are available before deciding what type of bond to purchase. If tax-sheltered retirement plans are not available, then discount or convertible bonds can receive consideration.

☐ Research Your Subject Before Buying

Lack of success in many security investments is often due the scant attention given such purchases prior to their ac- ¬ition. It is not uncommon for investors to buy $5000 to ᵖ00 worth of securities on the basis of a brief telephone ¬sation. These same investors would never purchase a ᵤᵤᵤ automobile or deposit $10,000 as downpayment on real estate on the basis of a short telephone conversation.

When a bond investor does wish to become better-informed prior to making commitments, it is often difficult to obtain reliable information from normal brokerage sources. Brokerage account executives (AEs) are not unlike insurance agents, in that many members of both professions make their recommendations primarily on the basis of resulting commissions rather than the best interests of their customers.

As a percent of the funds being invested, bond commission rates traditionally have been much lower than stock commission rates. This encourages AEs to concentrate their efforts in non-bond areas, consequently most AEs are poorly-informed concerning opportunities in bonds. Asking for their advice often results in the "blind leading the blind."

In order to become reasonably well-informed in the field of bonds, it may be necessary to conduct most of your own research. Sources of bond information are readily available in most libraries and brokerage offices. Chapter 7 discusses numerous factors which are important in the research of bonds and where to find such information.

It is also important that bond investors be aware of the various "gimmicks" which are periodically offered by the brokerage industry during periods of slow activity. This subject receives attention in Chapter 13.

☐ Locating Professional Assistance — The Bond Expert

Obtaining professional assistance is important for the beginning investor and can be quite helpful to experienced investors too. By becoming better-informed in the area of bonds, the investor can better judge the qualifications of securities salespersons.

The benefits of locating a bond expert are:

1. they can serve as an efficient and ready source of research information,
2. the investor will be notified concerning changing trends of interest rates,
3. the investor will be fully aware of attractive new bond issues and other opportunities which become available, and
4. specialists in bonds tend to be more conservative, a trait which is necessary for long-term success in any field of investing.

Due to the difficulty and importance of locating a bond expert, a comprehensive chapter (#14) is devoted to this subject.

☐ Bond Mutual Funds

Many persons prefer to use mutual funds for the management of their securitites. For a fee, the managements of bond mutual funds will make most of the major decisions for the investor. The investor must still decide *when* to purchase and sell shares of the mutual fund though, as most mutual funds have poor liquidity due to their vast holdings.

Investors should also realize that some sacrifice in yield is necessary when mutual funds are used. This is due to unavoidable management fees and minimum-size limitations of their holdings. A bond mutual fund cannot take advantage of bargains resulting from temporary price fluctuations unless a reasonable number of bonds are available (usually 100 or more). Chapter 11 provides more information concerning bond mutual funds.

The purchase of individual bonds by an investor will usually earn at least 10 percent more than yields available through most bond mutual funds. By gaining an understanding of bond securities, most investors should be able to manage their own bond investment programs and thereby maximize their returns.

*

Chapter 2

What Are Bonds?

To an *owner* of a bond certificate, the bond is evidence of a loan. For this loan, the bond owner receives both interest and the promise that the bond will be redeemed at its maturity.

To the *bond issuer* (a business corporation or government agency), the bond certificate is a legal obligation to fulfill specified interest and redemption terms. Essentially, persons who purchase bonds become creditors of these corporations and government agencies.

One of the attractions of a bond is its seniority to common and preferred stocks. The interest on bonds must be paid before dividends can be declared and paid.

*

BOND INTEREST PAYMENTS

Payment of bond interest is normally made at precise six month intervals. In a few instances, interest is paid monthly, quarterly, or even once a year.

☐ Interest Payment Dates

Most interest payment dates (IPDs) are scheduled on either the "first" or the "fifteenth" of the month. Whereas industrial bonds show no preference, the majority of utilities schedule their IPDs on the first of the month.

Prior to purchasing a bond, the buyer should check when its IPDs occur. These dates are easily obtained from a "Bond Guide" in the case of already-issued bonds or a final prospectus in the case of new-issues. Bonds which have been issued already are often referred to as "seasoned" bonds, whether they are listed or unlisted (over-the-counter).

In the "Bond Guide," IPDs are abbreviated using only the first letters of each payment month. Most bonds list two months, with the letter for the month of the bond's *final maturity* being capitalized. Following these two letters, there may be a number to designate the day of each month that the interest is paid. If there is no number, this means that interest is paid on the first of each month.

A bond's IPDs might appear as follows:

IPD	Definition
jJ	January 1st & July 1st
Fa	February 1st & August 1st
mS15	March 15th & September 15th
Ao29	April 29th & October 29th
mN	May 1st & November 1st
Jd15	June 15th & December 15th

Although IPDs in the "Bond Guide" are relatively simple to understand, bond customers may find that some brokerage salespersons have difficulty providing this information. Lack of a handy "Bond Guide" often contributes to the problem.

There are several reasons why a bond customer should inquire what the IPDs of potential bond purchases are. The main reason is to schedule interest payments according to an owner's preference. Rather than have all of one's bond income due on similar dates, many persons prefer to have IPDs of different bonds fall on various dates. Another important reason is to avoid large sums of *accrued interest* when seasoned bonds are purchased.

☐ Proration Of Interest

When a bond changes ownership, the seller receives interest up to, *but not including,* the settlement date of the transaction. On the settlement date, the new owner begins to earn interest on the bond. The settlement date is well *after* the execution date of a bond transaction. The execution date is the actual date on which the brokerage executes the order to buy or sell a bond. After an execution date, several days are required to prepare and deliver confirmation slips of the transaction to both the buyer and seller. A few more days are allowed for the seller to deliver the certificate to the selling brokerage, if necessary. Transactions of seasoned bonds normally have a settlement date which is 5 working days (or 7 calendar days) after the execution date. This usually works out to be the same day of the following week, unless a holiday is involved. This one week period also permits the buyer to conveniently arrange payment for the bond purchase.

Settlement dates for new-issue bonds may vary, but they usually approximate a week also. Settlement dates in the over-the-counter markets are more flexible and can be arranged according to the preferences of the buyer and seller. In the absence of contrary instructions, settlement dates are similar to those for listed bonds.

As a matter of course, most sellers of bonds sell somewhere between the IPD dates. In all of these cases, the interest is prorated between the buyer and seller in much the same manner that property taxes are prorated when real estate changes hands.

In the computation of prorated bond interest, there are three guidelines to follow:

1. a year is computed as having *360 days,*
2. all months are computed as being *30 days in length,* and
3. the settlement date of a transaction is *not* included when totaling the number of days since the last IPD.

The following explanation demonstrates how interest is prorated in bond transactions:

EXAMPLE:
The seller owns one bond with a 10% yield ($100 in yearly interest). The IPDs are June 1st and December 1st. The bond is sold with a settlement date of July 11th.

Step One: Divide yearly interest by days in year to get daily interest of bond.
$100 divided by 360 days
equals .27777, or
27.777¢ per day

Step Two: Total the days since the last IPD, omitting the settlement date.
June .... 30 days
July .... 10 days
Total............... 40 days
Step Three: Multiply daily interest by total days seller has owned bond since the last IPD.
27.777¢ times 40 days
equals $11.11.

☐ Registered Bonds

When bonds are registered, the bond certificate specifically states the name of either the owner or the owner's agent (a brokerage). When a customer's certificate is held at a brokerage and registered in the name of the brokerage, this form of ownership is referred to as "street name."

Therefore, the seller is entitled to $11.11 of *accrued interest* on the bond sale.

The above calculations are quite simple and require less than 10 seconds to compute with a calculator.

In the example, the $11.11 accrued interest is charged to the buyer of the bond and appears *as a cost* on the buyer's confirmation slip. Later, at the time of the next IPD (December 1st), the buyer will receive the full 6 months interest payment of $50 even though the buyer has held the bond for less than 6 months. To arrive at a figure which is reportable to the IRS (assuming the bond's interest is taxable), the buyer would subtract the $11.11 accrued interest from the six month interest figure of $50. Many persons mistakenly report the full 6 months interest payment to the IRS, forgetting to adjust this figure for any accrued interest which they may have been charged at the bond's purchase.

This system of prorating interest according to the holding period of the seller assures that a bondholder will receive all the interest which they are due. Bondholders have a distinct advantage over common stock and preferred stock holders, as the seller of stock receives nothing if they sell prior to a stock's ex-dividend date.

Holders of savings certificates at savings and loan institutions do not fare as well as bondholders either. If they wish to liquidate their certificates prior to a scheduled maturity date, they may be penalized as much as one-half a year's interest.

*

FORM OF OWNERSHIP

Bonds are issued in either registered or bearer form. In the past, some bond issues have permitted either type of ownership. Now most taxable bonds are issued in registered form and most tax-free municipal bonds are issued in bearer form.

When a registered bond is sold, it's usually necessary for the bond issuer to print a new certificate for the new owner. However, when a registered bond is in street name and changes hands, the issuance of a new certificate may not be necessary unless requested by the new owner.

Interest payments are mailed by the bond issuer to whoever is registered as the owner on the face of the certificate.

☐ Bearer Bonds

A bond certificate in bearer form has no owner name at all listed on its face. Whoever "bears" the bond certificate is considered its owner. These certificates require additional safekeeping due to their greater negotiability. When they exchange hands on a sale, the bond issuer is not notified of the transaction.

Owner of bearer bonds must detach interest coupons periodically from their bond certificates when interest is due to be paid. Most owners simply cash or deposit these pre-dated coupons at their local bank, for which there should be no charge.

*

BOND YIELDS

The interest rate or yield of a bond can be expressed in several different ways, which often leads to some confusion.

When a newly-issued bond is selling at par ($1000), its coupon rate, current yield, and yield to maturity are all the same.

☐ Coupon Rate

The term "coupon rate" is used to describe either a bond's percentage yield at par *or* its dollar amount of yearly interest. If a bond's description is

"Atlantic Telephone...9½%...1986"

its coupon is 9½% or $95 per year.

When a bond salesperson tells us that a new-issue bond has a "9½% interest rate," they are probably stating its coupon rate (assuming the bond is to be issued exactly at par).

☐ Current Yield

After a bond has been issued, it begins to fluctuate according to its demand and supply, in addition to changes in the general level of interest rates.

If general interest rates increase measurably, the forementioned Atlantic Telephone 9½% 1986 bond would then decline in price. Its yield would change also and might be expressed in either of two ways:

1. by its current yield, or
2. by its yield to maturity.

The *current yield* is obtained by dividing a bond's coupon rate by its current price. If the Atlantic Telephone bond declined to $940, a current yield figure of 10.1% would be obtained by dividing $95 by $940. In determining a bond's attractiveness, most owners of bonds consider the current yield to be the most important yield figure.

☐ Yield To Maturity

The "yield to maturity" of a bond takes into consideration the eventual maturity of the bond (when it will be redeemed at par). The person who purchases a bond at $940 and holds it until maturity will enjoy a small capital gain of $60. When one wishes to compute a bond's yield to maturity, this capital gain must be amortized over the remaining life of the bond.

The securities industry has devised a complicated, computerized method of arriving at various yields to maturity, which are listed in manuals called "Bond Yield Tables."

The following computations provide a reasonable approximation of how yields to maturity are obtained. Two separate yields (A and B) are computed, which are then averaged to arrive at a yield to maturity.

EXAMPLE: A bond with a 9½% coupon, maturing in 6 years is purchased at $940.

Step One: Subtract the purchase price ($940) from par ($1000), to arrive at a discount of $60.

Step Two: Divide the discount ($60) by the remaining years (6) of the bond to obtain an annualized capital gain ($10).

Step Three: Add the annual capital gain ($10) to the yearly coupon ($95) to obtain a total yearly return of $105.

Step Four: Divide the yearly return ($105) by the purchase price ($940) to obtain *Yield "A", or 11.17%.*

Step Five: Subtract the annual capital gain ($10) from par, resulting in $990.

Step Six: Divide the yearly return ($105) by $990 to obtain *Yield "B", or 10.61%.*

Step Seven: Average Yields "A" and "B", resulting in a *10.89% yield to maturity.*

Many bond owners prefer to compute the yield to maturity using only the first four steps. This is acceptable when one's purpose is simply to compare various bond alternatives.

*

BOND QUOTES AND FLUCTUATIONS

Bond prices vary daily just as common stock prices do, however their percentage fluctuations are usually far less than those of common stocks.

Major newspapers and "The Wall Street Journal" are common sources of bond quotes, which appear in abbreviated form. In newspaper tabulations, the market price of a bond is shown as a percentage of its par value, thus a bond selling at $985 would be listed as 98½.

The following list of bond quotes is typical of how these prices appear. An explanation is also included:

	Cur Yld	Close	Net Chg	Explanation
				Amer. Tel&Tel 8⅜% 2007
ATT8⅜s07	9.2	94⅛	+ ⅛	*Close* $941.25. *Net Change:* + $1.25.
				Amfac 5¼% 1994, convertible.
Amfac5¼94	cv	68½	− ⅜	*Close:* $685. *Net Change:* −$3.75
				Ampex 5½% 1994, convertible.
Ampx5½94	cv	69	+ ¾	*Close:* $69. *Net Change:* +$7.50.
				Anheuser 6% 1992
Anhr6s92	7.2	83½	− ½	*Close:* $835. *Net Change:* −$5.00
				Appalachian Power 10½% 1984
AppP10½84	10.4	101¼	+ ¾	*Close:* $1012.50. *Net Change:* +$7.50.
				ARCO Pipeline 8% 1982
Arco8s82	8.3	96½	− ⅛	*Close:* $965. *Net Change:* −$1.25.

The group of numbers which appears immediately after the abbreviated corporate name reveals the coupon rate and year of maturity of each bond. The letter "s" has no meaning; it simply serves to separate the coupon and maturity figures whenever fractions do not appear in the coupon rate.

The second column lists either the current yield of the bond or the letters "cv" when the bond is convertible into stock. A convertible feature often accounts for a lower than normal yield, in comparison to other listed yields of equal quality.

The figures in the last two columns provide the daily closing price and any fluctuation from the previous closing price. When no transactions occur in a bond, it is not listed in daily quotes. There are many bonds which appear each day, however it is not unusual for many of the listed bonds to appear only periodically.

□ Interpreting Bond Quotes

Converting bond quotes into real numbers is a simple procedure. When bonds are quoted in round percentages, their equivalent values in whole numbers can be derived by adding a "zero" to the end of the figure:

Bond Quote	Real Value
86	$860
72	$720
98	$980

Most of the time, bond quotes will contain a fractional amount. In bonds, such figures are fractions of *a $10 unit*, and are listed in *eighths* of this unit. To convert fractional yield figures into numerical equivalents and dollar values of a bond, the following scale may be helpful:

Fractional Amount	Equivalent Number	Dollar Value Of Bond
⅛	.125	$1.25
¼	.250	$2.50
⅜	.375	$3.75
½	.500	$5.00
⅝	.625	$6.25
¾	.750	$7.50
⅞	.875	$8.75

Examples of bond quotes with fractions and their dollar values are:

Bond Quote	Dollar Value
84½	$845.00
96⅝	$966.25

☐ Points & Basis Points

Traders in bonds often refer to the previously-discussed $10 unit of trading as a "point." Hence, 2 points would be $20, and 3½ points would be equivalent to $35.

Not to be confused with this usuage of the word "point" is the term "basis points." When professionals use the term "basis points," they are referring to the *difference* between particular percentage yields. Each *one-hundredth of a percentage point* is equal to one basis point. For example, if bond "A" yields 9.25% and bond "B" yields 9.75%, the difference in their yields would be *50 basis points*. Or, if bond "C" yields 8.30% and bond "D" yields 9.40%, the difference would be *110 basis points*.

There is virtually no relationship between these two terms. A "point" refers to a *ten dollar unit* value of bonds, and "basis points" refers to the difference between percentage yields of bonds. Understanding the difference between these two terms often distinquishes the "bond expert" from ordinary stockbrokers, although some stockbrokers may understand neither term.

*

LISTED AND OVER-THE-COUNTER QUOTES

Prior to entering an order to buy or sell a bond, an investor should always *request* a quote on the bond. In the majority of cases, this will reveal the exact terms at which a bond can be traded.

☐ "Bid & Ask" Quotes

Bond quotes are frequently furnished as a result of requesting a "Bid & Ask." This simply means that the investor wishes to know the highest current bid (buy price) and the lowest current offer (sell price) of a particular bond.

For example, a potential seller of 10 Atlantic Telephone 10% 1992 bonds requests a "Bid & Ask," and the brokerage then obtains a quote of:

"93½ to 94."

This means that the highest bid to buy this bond is currently $935, while the lowest selling price is at $940. On the basis of this information, our potential bond seller should *not yet enter an order*.

☐ "Quote & Size" Quotes

As our investor wishes to sell 10 bonds, it is important to obtain data concerning *how many* bonds the highest bidder is willing to purchase at the $935 price. It may also be important to know how many bonds the lowest seller has for sale, as this is a competing order.

To obtain the volume (or size) of the current "Bid & Ask," the astute investor will initially request a "Quote & Size." In our example, the "Quote & Size" might be:

"93½ to 94, 15 by 25."

This means that the highest bid at 93½ is a bid to purchase 15 bonds. Twenty-five (25) bonds are being offered for sale at 94.

The seller of 10 Atlantic Telephone bonds could sell immediately at a price of $935, to whomever is bidding for 15 bonds at this price. Or an order could be entered to sell the 10 bonds at 94, in which case the order would not be executed until the prior 25 bonds have been sold at 94, or withdrawn.

The brokerage might advise the seller that the latest trading price of the bond is at 93¾, or $937.50. This may be a reasonable price to attempt a sale also. There are numerous options available to the *informed* investor.

Most brokerage offices have quote machines which can instantly furnish "Quote & Sizes." Other offices may have to wire their main New York office to obtain such information.

□ Avoiding Wide Spreads

In some instances there may be an unusually wide spread between the bid and ask prices of a bond quote. This may be due to a temporary scarcity of orders in a particular bond issue, or a bond may trade occasionally with wide quotes due to having relatively few bonds outstanding. In such cases, a quote might be:

"92 to 95"

with a latest trade at 95. A person placing an order to sell immediately *without first checking* the quote of the bond might be greatly disappointed to receive only $920 for their bonds when the previous trade was at $950.

This is another good reason why buyers and sellers of bonds should request a quote prior to entering their orders. A few brokerages firms and almost all 'bond experts" will inform their customers when there is a wide disparity between the latest trade in a bond and a potential execution price.

□ Over-The-Counter Quotes

In the over-the-counter (OTC) market, wide price spreads are normal. Most of the unlisted bonds with which the public comes into contact are tax-free municipal bonds. As mentioned earlier, the assistance of a "bond expert" as a broker can be invaluable for both inexperienced and experienced investors; and the field of unlisted bonds is one of the most important areas where professional assistance is vital.

The unlisted bond market provides *more limited* information to the prospective bond owner for several reasons. There is a lack of a major central marketplace where information can be efficiently gathered. New electronic reporting services can provide rapid quotes on OTC bonds in many cases, however the prices furnished may or may not be "competitive." Volume in OTC bonds is relatively low also, which may not be convenient for buyers or sellers.

☐ Brokerages Providing Quotes As A Principal

Quite often, a quote is "created" by a brokerage for the convenience of the seller (or the brokerage). This means that the brokerage makes an offer to buy the bonds directly from their selling customer. In doing so, the brokerage is acting as a "principal" instead of an agent for their customer.

If the brokerage does purchase the bonds from a customer, they hope to re-sell such securities at a profit later. In order to do so, the brokerage will naturally attempt to buy the bonds as cheaply as possible. This is not an abnormal intention, however individuals should be fully informed when their brokerage is acting as a "principal" in a transaction. Current regulations require that customers be so informed, although in some cases this notice is provided *after* the transaction in a manner which many customers may not understand. Without an explanation of the term, the confirmation slip will state "principal" somewhere on its face.

When selling unlisted bonds, it is important that investors request quotes from several different brokerages to ensure that their bonds are being sold at a competitive price.

*

MATURITIES OF BONDS

All bonds which are being currently issued are scheduled for retirement by redemption *or* at their maturity. Redemption prior to maturity depends on each bond's call provisions.

☐ Length Of Bond Maturities.

Bonds are issued in varying maturities according to the needs of the bond issuer and conditions in the bond market.

In normal markets, a corporation can dictate the precise maturity of its new-issues. If funds are required for the long-term, bonds may be issued for 20 to 35 years. Intermediate maturities may range from 10 to 20 years, with short-term issues having a maturity of less than 10 years. Debt issues maturing in less than 10 years are commonly called "notes" instead of bonds. It is not unusual for a corporation to issue both short-term and long-term debt simultaneously.

Notes generally carry a lower interest rate as they are considered somewhat safer due to their shorter life. In recent years though, there have been several market periods when the longer term bonds carried the lower rates due to:

1. scarcity of long term issues, and
2. corporate preferences for shorter term debt during periods of exceptionally high interest rates.

☐ Call Provisions

Most bonds give their issuer the option of redeeming their bonds prior to maturity. A bond issuer may retire bond debt early for a number of reasons, including:

1. to refund (re-finance) their bond debt at a lower interest rate,
2. to eliminate debt when funds are available for its retirement, or
3. to redeem bonds in an orderly progression according to previous sinking fund provisions (to be explained).

When a bond issuer does exercise its right to redeem a bond earlier than maturity, it may be required to pay a penalty to affected bond holders in the form of a premium over and above the bond's par value. The size of this premium varies according to the length of time the "call" occurs since the bond has been originally issued. In the first year that a call option can be exercised, the premium is usually at its maximum.

Generally speaking, utility bond issues are not callable until they have been outstanding at least 5 years. Industrial bonds usually cannot be called for refunding purposes during their first 10 years.

In the past, the amount of premium payable if a bond was called during its first year of eligibility usually amounted to the equivalent of a full year's interest. A number of recent corporate issues, beginning in 1979, have begun to offer only a half-year's interest as the first year premium. With each succeeding year after the first year of call eligibility, the premium declines somewhat. The period during which a premium remains payable upon early redemption ranges from 6 to 7 years to as long as 30 years in some cases. Utilities normally offer longer periods during which premiums are payable than industrial corporations.

Determining the general call provisions of a bond is possible by reviewing the bond's description in a "Bond Guide." More precise figures appear on the back of the bond certificate, within the final prospectus of the bond issue, or in reference volumes found in most brokerage offices. Reference books published by Standard & Poor's Corporation furnish this data in encyclopedic form. Prospective buyers of listed bonds must use either the final prospectus (when available) or these reference books.

If a new-issue bond is being considered, this type of information is usually not available until the day of the new-issue's sale. Approximate figures can be obtained by reviewing similar new-issues which have been recently brought to market.

☐ "Open Market" Purchases For Redemption Purposes

Currently, corporations are permitted to purchase their own bonds in the market place for redemption purposes. When a bond issuer's debt is selling *below par,* the bond issuer may choose to retire bonds at this discounted cost. From the standpoint of corporate profits, this is preferable to paying $1000 par value to retire bonds. When such purchases are made, the issuer generates a profit, which is the difference between the discounted cost and $1000 par value. This "legal loophole" allows corporations to circumvent the normal procedure of paying bondholders full par value upon retirement of bonds.

In 1979 a legal suit was filed to prevent U.S. government agencies from redeeming their bonds in this manner. If this lawsuit is successful, perhaps it will eventually benefit holders of corporate bonds also. Bond issuers and the brokerage industry repeatedly state to prospective bond buyers that bonds are *redeemable at $1000 par value upon their maturity.* This should be a totally true statement. Bonds which have been previously purchased at a discount by their issuer cannot be redeemed at par upon maturity.

☐ Calling Bonds Which Are Selling Over Par

Another questionable corporate practice is the call for redemption of bonds at par while they are *selling well over par* in the marketplace.

After a certain number of years, a corporation may be required to redeem a specific number of bonds every year in order to satisfy sinking fund requirements. Written notification (call) of such redemption is provided to bondholders, whose bonds are drawn by lot. Quite often (during periods of low interest rates), these bonds may be selling in the open market at prices well above $1000 par value.

When a bondholder receives such a redemption notice, they have no choice but to turn the bond in for redemption as no further interest will be paid on "redeemed" bonds. For example, let us assume that a long-term bondholder has 5 Atlantic Telephone bonds which are currently selling at $1080 each. Atlantic Telephone notifies this bondholder that one of the 5 bonds is being called at par. The bondholder has an *instant loss* of $80 on the called bond.

Since corporations now have the right to buy their bonds for redemption purposes when they are selling below par, it does not seem appropriate that they also should be permitted to generate "instant losses" among their bondholders by redeeming bonds below their open market value.

A more equitable solution would be to require bond issuers to redeem bonds selling over par at their fair market value. This, of course, would generate a slight loss for the corporation which might be balanced against profits generated when open market purchases are made below par. Perhaps, legislation will correct this inequity within the near future.

In the meanwhile, potential bond buyers should be cautious when purchasing any bond over $1000 in price. If the bonds are currently callable at par, their owner may be instantly disappointed.

*

TYPES OF BONDS

Bonds vary according to their type of issuer and the extent to which the issuer guarantees the bond. In the following discussion, only taxable bonds are described. Tax-free bonds are discussed in Chapter 12.

☐ Debentures

The most common type of taxable bond is called a "debenture." Holders of debentures are general creditors of the corporate bond issuer. All corporate assets and property which are not otherwise pledged secure debenture bonds.

☐ Senior And Subordinated Bonds

When a company has more than one bond issue outstanding, they often pre-designate the seniority of their issues. A subordinated bond will be second to a senior issue in the payment of interest and eventual redemption. Seniority of bonds becomes important only when a company faces serious financial difficulties which may force it out of business.

☐ Sinking Fund Bonds

The term "sinking fund" denotes that provision has been made to retire a specific number of bonds each year, until final maturity. Bonds to be retired are usually chosen by random lot and may be redeemed:

1. at par value,
2. at a premium over par according to the bond's call conditions, or
3. at a discount below par (through open-market purchases).

Sinking fund payments are usually made by the corporate issuer to a trust company or trustee bank, which becomes responsible for redemption of the bonds. The redemption of bonds by a sinking fund normally commences 5 to 10 years after issuance of the bonds.

☐ First Mortgage Bonds

When a bond issuer wishes to add additional security to a new bond issue, they can designate particular corporate property as collateral for the bond issue. This may result in a slightly lower coupon rate for the bond.

Supposedly, if the bond issuer defaults on either interest or principal payments, the mortgaged property can be sold to satisfy the bond's requirements. In reality, there may be little demand for production facilities of a defunct company. Nevertheless, this is one of the more desirable forms for a bond issue.

☐ Income Bonds

Occasionally, a bond will be issued with the condition that interest is payable only if the corporation operates at a profit. This, of course, is not a very attractive condition to the average bond investor. Such bonds are rarely issued today, and those which are should not be seriously considered by investors.

☐ Equipment Trust Certificates

These certificates are evidence of investor ownership in "rolling stock" leased by a transportation-oriented corporation. Rolling stock includes freight cars and locomotives, aircraft, or truck trailers.

This form of bond is issued in the name of the transportation company which leases the rolling stock from an owner bank. A *second* bank normally acts as the trustee bank for certificate holders. As lease payments are made to the owner bank, necessary funds are forwarded to the second bank in order to pay interest and provide for the periodic redemption of such certificates.

Since the collateral behind these certificates is readily transferred to another transportation company's use, this type of bond is considered quite secure (as long as demand for the equipment involved is good).

These certificates are frequently issued in *serial form,* meaning that they are to be redeemed in much the same manner as sinking fund bonds. The difference is that serial bonds are redeemed *at par* and *by particular serial number* in an orderly, predictable fashion. For this reason, serial bonds are quite popular with institutional investors. When legislation is passed to improve redemption procedures for bonds, this form of redemption would provide the most equitable procedure for public bondholders.

☐ Convertible Bonds

Owners of convertible bonds have the option of exchanging their bonds for a specific number of common shares of the same corporation. The number of shares is determined by dividing the bond's *conversion price* into par ($1000). The back of the "Bond Guide" provides both conversion prices (under the 'Price Per Share' column) and the number of shares into which each bond can be converted.

The *conversion value* of a bond is obtained by multiplying the stock's price by the number of shares into which the bond is convertible. Convertible bonds normally are priced higher than their conversion values due to the attraction of their convertibility. This excess over conversion value is called its "premium."

When the price of the common stock is above the bond's conversion price, the bond will sell in excess of $1000 and will fluctuate proportionally with the common stock.

When the price of the common stock is below the bond's conversion price, the value of the bond is influenced by a second factor — the general level of interest rates. The bond may then assume an "investment value," meaning it may be valued according to the desirability of its current yield instead of its potential for conversion.

Due to the conversion privilege, the coupon rate of most convertible bonds ranges from one-third to one-half *less* than similar quality bonds which are not convertible.

□ "Flower Bonds"

There are a number of U.S. Treasury bonds which can be acquired at *substantial discounts below par* and then used to pay Federal estate taxes at their *full par value*.

Due to this tax "loophole," these bonds are often purchased shortly before the death of an individual with a sizeable estate. In late 1979, the average price of these "flower bonds" was $830, which at that time afforded a tax savings of $170 per bond.

The following table lists various issues of flower bonds maturing after 1982, with their approximate values in late 1979.

Issue		Maturity (if not previously called)	Approximate Price per $1000 of face value
3¼%	1978-83	6/15/83	$868
4¼%	1975-85	5/15/85	831
3¼%	1985	5/15/85	828
4¼%	1987-92	8/15/92	823
4%	1988-93	2/15/93	838
4 1/8%	1989-94	5/15/94	822
3½%	1990	2/15/90	812
3%	1995	2/15/95	826
3½%	1998	11/15/98	822

Quotes on flower bonds appear in "The Wall Street Journal" in the 'Treasury Issues' column. Prior to purchasing these bonds for Federal estate purposes, a competent tax advisor should be consulted to assess the potential savings these securities can offer.

There are numerous other, less-important bond forms; a number of which are discussed in Chapter 13.

*

RATINGS OF BONDS

Several private firms provide ratings to bond issuers, for a fee. The major rating services are Standard & Poor's Corporation and Moody's Investor's Services. Their ratings provide a *very* general guide to bond buyers. One should never totally rely on ratings as a guide to purchases, as these services usually do not know of major corporate developments any earlier than other readers of financial news. On frequent occasions, they have been slow in changing ratings, even after adverse corporate news has been reported.

☐ Rating Levels
The quality of any bond is measured by the safety of both its interest and principal payments. The two rating services offer similar rating systems, although their "letter" designations differ somewhat. The table below lists comparable ratings of the major services, with 'AAA' being the highest rating of both services.

Standard & Poor's Corporation		Moody's Investor Services
AAA	. . . .	AAA
AA	. . . .	AA
A	. . . .	A
BBB	. . . .	BAA
BB	. . . .	BA
B	. . . .	B
CCC	. . . .	CAA
CC	. . . .	CA
C	. . . .	C

The rating letters used by Moody's Investor's Services may cause some confusion for beginning investors, as the first letter of several of their ratings is combined with letters used in other higher ratings. Fortunately, the "Bond Guide" found most frequently at brokerage offices is published by the other rating service and offers clearer designations.

References describing the meanings of these ratings are relatively inconcise. Standard & Poor's ratings use the following terms to describe the "capacity to pay interest and repay principal."

Ratings		Description
AAA	....	"extremely strong"
AA	....	"very strong"
A	....	"strong"
BBB	....	"adequate"
BB, B, CCC & CC	....	"predominantly speculative" in increasing degrees

Their 'C' and 'D' ratings are reserved for bonds which are no longer paying interest. 'C' is for income bonds and 'D' is for all other types of bonds.

An 'NR' rating means that the bond is not rated and may be given to a bond for one of several reasons:

1. no rating has been requested by the bond issuer,
2. insufficient information is available on which to base a rating, or
3. the rating service does not furnish ratings on this particular type of bond.

Standard & Poor's Corporation also assigns Plus (+) or Minus (-) modifications to some ratings ranging from 'AA' to 'BB' in order to designate a bond's relative standing within these categories.

The above ratings are of more importance to institutional investors than individuals, as government regulations and the bylaws of many institutions restrict their purchases to specific rating categories. Banks are prevented from purchasing bonds below the 'BBB' level by the Comptroller of the Currency, a federal government agency.

☐ How Are Ratings Obtained?

To obtain a rating, bond issuers or their underwriting brokerage groups must pay fees to the rating services. These fees range from $1000 to $10,000 for tax-free municipal bonds and from $500 to $15,000 for taxable corporate bonds.

*

BONDS AS COLLATERAL

One of the advantages of placing capital into bond investments is the ease and favorable terms in which bonds can be borrowed upon.

The maximum percentage that can be borrowed on bonds is controlled by the Federal Reserve. Normally, most corporate bonds have had a loan value of 65 percent in recent years. Convertible bonds, being more speculative, have had a loan value of 50 percent. Bond securities issued by federal government agencies have had loan values as high as 90 percent. Tax-free municipal bonds also have a high loan value; however, one loses the right to deduct interest charges on the loan amount when municipal bonds are collateralized (discussed in detail in Chapter 12).

☐ Borrowing At Your Bank

When we have reason to borrow at a bank, one of the first questions asked by the banker is "what collateral can you furnish?" Banks are quite willing to receive bonds as collateral for two basic reasons:

1. bonds are readily marketable, and
2. bonds fluctuate relatively little compared to stocks.

At the bank, the borrower may be asked to sign a form called a "bond power," which is the equivalent of signing the back of the bond certificate. If necessary, this permits the bank to transfer title of the bond to the bank. Normally, the certificate is promptly returned to the owner when the loan is eliminated.

When a bond power is not utilized, the bank will ask the owner to endorse the back of the certificate. When the loan is paid off, it is then necessary to obtain a new certificate as endorsed certificates are negotiable. The bank should arrange for the issuance of a new certificate.

☐ Borrowing At A Brokerage

When it's convenient to borrow at a brokerage, the interest charged is often less than at a bank and far less paperwork is required. Brokerage loan rates are usually set slightly above the prime rate charged by banks, and are automatically adjusted whenever the prime rate changes.

More favorable loan rates are available from a brokerage as it is anticipated that the bond owner will do "business" with the brokerage. As long as the customer maintains somewhat of an active account, these loans can be maintained indefinitely. When no transactions have occurred for a lengthy period, the client may be asked to transfer the loan to a bank.

Borrowers at a brokerage are not required to make periodic monthly payments in order to reduce their loans. Interest charges are computed on a monthly basis and simply increase the size of the loan; however, a few clients may wish to deposit monthly checks to cover approximate interest charges. These loans can be reduced or eliminated whenever the client wishes to deposit funds into their account (or by selling securities).

*

Chapter 3

Understanding Interest Rates

The prices of bonds fluctuate in inverse proportion to changes in interest rates. If the average coupon rate provided by new-issue bonds *declines* by 5 percent, then seasoned bonds might be expected to *increase* in value by 5 percent; and vice versa. Understanding why yields offered by new-issue bonds are constantly changing may assist the bond buyer in making more timely purchases.

Bond investors should watch changes in general interest rates for indications of new trends. The sooner a trend can be recognized, the quicker an investor can take appropriate positions.

As in the stock market, everyone tries to be first. A characteristic of general stock movements is that they usually occur much quicker than movements in the bond market. As a result, many stock market trends are *established and over with* before stock investors have had an opportunity to profit from them (excepting specialists and a few professionals). Since there is normally a *longer time span* during changes in interest rates, bond investors have a greater opportunity to make profitable decisions. Another advantage enjoyed by bond investors is the fact that most bonds of *comparable quality* tend to act similarly in each interest rate cycle. This makes the choice of specific bond investments much easier.

*

WHAT CAUSES BOND INTEREST RATES TO FLUCTUATE?

There are numerous factors which influence the direction of bond interest rates. The study of these factors and their varying influence on interest rates is more of an "art" than a science (otherwise economists might all be wealthy).

Bond interest rates change as a direct result of how other closely-related interest rates fluctuate. These other rates include:

1. 90-day U.S. Treasury bill yields,
2. 3-year U.S. Treasury note yields,
3. the federal funds rate,
4. the prime rate at banks,
5. yields on certificates of deposit, and
6. commercial paper rates.

Unusual demand for money in different sectors of the economy can result in significant increases or decreases in one or more of the above rates. Changes in these rates are closely monitored by both government and corporate leaders who are responsible for managing most of the funds providing these yields. Quite often, a "domino-effect" is noticed when one of these rates starts moving rapidly. Unfortunately, there is no consistent pattern which would permit us to assign an order of importance to the above rates. They assume varying importance with each succeeding interest rate cycle.

Most of these interest rates are quite visible, while a few are seldom mentioned except in financial news sources such as "Barrons" or the "The Wall Street Journal."

☐ Government-Controlled Interest Rates

One of the more closely-observed rates is the yield offered at weekly auctions of 90-day U.S. Treasury bills. These auctions are held on Mondays and reported in the major newspapers on Tuesdays. The sale of U.S. Treasury bills is a major tool of the federal government for:

1. influencing the availability of credit through the banking system, and
2. financing the deficit in the national budget.

Weekly changes in this rate can vary from a few basis points to more than 100 basis points (a full percentage point). Since auctions of 90-day Treasury bills take place on a regular schedule, they are easily monitored for new interest rate trends. The government often attempts to drive other interest rates up or down with this tool. However, in the process of financing heavy deficits, government efforts to use this tool to lower other interest rates are often relatively ineffective.

Another important government-controlled interest rate is that of 3-year U.S. Treasury notes. Being longer term government issues, these notes provide a better indication of future returns on other long term bond issues. There are numerous other forms of government borrowing which in 1978 totalled close to $55 billion. The significance of this federal borrowing is considerable, as in 1978 it equalled the total volume of new corporate borrowing (26½ billion) and new financing by municipalities ($29 billion).

In addition, the federal government controls the yields that banks pay for their own short term borrowings (usually overnight) through the *federal funds rate.* The Federal Reserve sets this rate, which is rarely discussed in any media.

Note: If you wish to impress your banker when negotiating a loan, ask "Where the federal funds rate is expected to move next?" Your banker may or may not be aware of the latest change (as you should be), however your banker will be impressed with your apparent knowledge of the banking business. The author once obtained a long-term loan which was 200 basis points below the going rate via this technique.

☐ Government Reactions, Actions, And Other Mistakes

Many economic realists assert that attempts by agencies of the federal government to influence general interest rates are more the result of *reactions* to various economic trends than the application of positive actions to influence economic forces. As often as the government is accused of solely reacting to events, they are also accused of inaction. A difficulty faced by government economists is that there is no way to accurately measure the precise cause-and-effect relationships between general economic forces, however much some economists may wish us to believe otherwise.

An example of "underthink" on the part of government economists was exhibited in attempts to control inflation during the late 1970's by *increasing interest rates*. An editorial in the December 9, 1979 issue of the "Los Angeles Times" entitled 'Fed's Interest Rate Moves May Add To Inflation' explains:

"As business costs, they become consumer costs, and inflate retail prices, whether purchasers use cash or credit. Because today's long-term interest charges will have to be paid out of tomorrow's prices, long-term rates are not only an anticipation but a partial guarantee, of future inflation."

What this type of government policy does to general prices paid by ordinary consumers is seen each time we go shopping or make mortgage payments on recently-purchased homes.

☐ Private Sector Interest Rates

Government ,manipulation of U.S. Treasury offerings, the federal funds rate, and many other controls places pressure on three important interest rates within the private sector of the economy:

1. the prime rate,
2. certificate of deposit rates, and
3. commercial paper rates.

The prime rate is usually described as the bank loan rate made available only to a bank's best customers. According to economists and their textbooks, all other borrowers must pay higher rates according to the risk the bank must assume in making their loans. Actually, ordinary citizens can obtain this rate too; if they exercise care during loan negotiations. It is very important *to know* your banker.

Many large investors are familiar with the yields offered by *certificates of deposit* at banks and thrift institutions. These deposits require both minimum amounts and time periods.

Commercial paper is just what it sounds like: borrowings by business corporations. The average maturity of these loans is 2 to 3 months and the normal minimum amount is $250,000, although lesser amounts are available from some sources.

These six "other" interest rates, to an important extent, determine the yields within the bond market. The only way they can be reasonably monitored is by a daily reading of "The Wall Street Journal." Other publications such as "Barrons," "Business Week," and "Forbes" also assist. When the bond investor is unable or unwilling to assume this reading responsibility, they should assure that their account executive is well-informed in this area.

Comparative levels of these interest rates, plus corporate and municipal yields, are listed below.

	End Of The Year		
	1977	1978	1979
90-day U.S. Treasury Bills ...	6.15%	9.34%	12.00%
3-year Treasury Notes	7.39	9.59	11.70
Federal Funds Rate	6.53	10.84	13.62
Prime Rate	7.75	11.75	15.25
Certificates Of Deposit			
(90 day)	6.75	10.80	13.50
Commercial Paper (90 day) ...	6.83	10.69	13.25
Telephone Bond New-Issues ..	8.50	9.45	10.50
Municipal Bond New-Issues ..	5.66	6.61	7.25

51

☐ International Events

The unexpected in the way of international events (political, economic, weather, etc.) can significantly influence the level of interest rates in the United States.

An example was the Arab-Israeli conflict of 1972, the results of which strengthened the oil-marketing organization of Arab oil producers. Consequent oil price escalations led to both a serious recession and the highest interest rates in the United States *since the Civil War*. The opportunity to purchase bonds with unprecedented high yields was a blessing to bond buyers. Continuing Middle East problems contributed to similar high interest rates in the late 1970's.

It is extremely unfortunate that human suffering occurs in the form of wars, droughts, and other catastrophic events; however, it is a foolish investor who fails to recognize and adjust to the unusual demands which such events can place on domestic and foreign economies. If we cannot prevail on political leaders to prevent such events where possible, then we should protect ourselves from their ill effects.

Many astute investors place their funds into short-term bond maturities at the outset of these events and later transfer their funds into longer term maturities when interest rates appear to be peaking.

☐ Consumer Spending & Saving Habits

Demand for consumer credit expanded by $48 billion in 1978, almost as much as the federal government's credit grew that year. A major portion of consumer credit was for the purchase of America's favorite toy — the new automobile. The level of new car sales is a very important factor for bond investors to follow. A slackening of demand for new cars, combined with several other negative factors, can lead to both a recession and lower interest rates. New car sales are announced at 10-day intervals. Although local newspapers often announce these figures, they seldom reveal conditions such as sales contests and holidays which reduce the reliability of reported figures. "The Wall Street Journal" *does* reveal such information in their car sales reports.

In 1978 other consumer borrowing for home purchases totaled $95 billion, the heaviest demand for credit in the entire economy. This explains why the level of new mortgage debt is often discussed in economic news. The tremendous demand for credit by these buyers influences all other interest rates.

The degree that individuals save instead of spend their incomes has a significant effect on lendable funds at banks, savings and loans, and other thrift institutions. During a period of above-average savings, interest rates tend to be lower. When the public chooses to spend more freely, not only does increased demand for consumer credit occur, but there are less funds on deposit at lending institutions to meet this consumer demand.

Increased or decreased public deposits at saving and loans are announced on a monthly basis and should be noted by bond investors. In past periods, high interest rates tended to reduce consumer demand for home loans, however this was not the case in the late 1970s as buyers of homes seemed more concerned with escalating home prices than high loan rates.

☐ Corporate Borrowing Requirements

Corporate borrowing in 1978 was $26½ billion, $4½ billion less than in 1977. Many analysts attributed this decline to corporate reluctance to borrow at high interest rates which prevailed during 1978.

During periods of high interest rates, a reduced supply of new corporate bonds often has the effect of keeping bond yields relatively low in relation to other interest rates. In the previous table which compared interest rates from 1977 to 1979, the increase in yields of telephone bond offerings from 1977 to 1979 was *only 24%,* while 5 of the other interest rates increased *more than 90 percent.* Telephone bond new-issues are approximately 25 percent of all taxable bond new-issues.

Volume of new corporate bond offerings is generally reported on a monthly basis in "The Wall Street Journal." Investors should be aware of changes in this volume, as varying supply of new bonds can have an immediate effect on bond yields.

☐ Municipal Borrowing Needs

The credit requirement of states, counties, cities, and their many political sub-divisions have steadily increased almost every year, until 1979.

A non-economic factor which occurred in California greatly reduced the willingness of state and other local politicians to continue expanding municipal bond debt. The success of the Jarvis-Gann tax initiative in 1978 served notice to nationwide political leadership that uncontrolled municipal borrowing was undesirable and unacceptable. As a result, new-issues of tax-free bonds in 1979 declined by approximately 20 percent, a major change in this market. Local newspapers outside of California may have given little notice to the success of this tax initiative, which is another reason for regularly reviewing a *national source* of political/financial news.

*

WHY INTEREST RATES VARY AMONG BONDS

Several factors dictate yields among various bonds, including quality ratings, maturities, redemption features, convertible options, size of the bond's issue, and the nature of the bond issuer's business.

☐ Quality Ratings

Generally speaking, the higher the rating of a bond, the lower will be its interest rate. However, there are many exceptions.

Quite often, a bond in a preferred industry will not yield as much as a higher-rated bond in a less desirable industry. Since the energy problems of the 1970s, numerous industrial bonds have been successfully marketed with lower coupons than other higher-rated utility offerings.

Another important factor causing some higher-rated utility bonds to yield more than industrial bonds is a varying call option. During periods of high interest rates, investors often prefer the 10-year call protection usually provided by industrial bonds *rather than* the 5-year protection offered by utility bond issues.

The *yield spread* between various grades of bonds constantly changes according to supply and demand conditions. The following table is an example of what spreads might be among different grades of bonds.

Ratings	Spreads
AAA to AA	1/4 of 1%
AA to A	1/2 of 1%
A to BBB	7/8 of 1%
BBB to BB, B	1½%

☐ Differing Maturities

It is normal for longer term bonds to have higher yields, as these bonds involve a longer risk to the lender's funds. However, as mentioned in the previous chapter, a temporary shortage of long-term new-issues during a period of *extremely high* interest rates may drive the yields on more plentiful short-term offering to higher levels.

In normal bond markets (and what is "normal" may vary with each interest rate cycle), we might find the following yields among similar quality bonds of differing maturities.

Years Of Maturity		Possible Yields
5	. . . .	7½%
10	. . . .	8½%
15 +	. . . .	9 to 10%

☐ Convertible Options

In daily bond listings, each convertible bond is so designated in order to prevent misunderstandings concerning what may appear as an excessively low yield compared to other equal quality bonds. When a convertible bond's conversion price is close to the market price of its common stock, the yield of the bond may become *irrelevant*. Decreased attractiveness of such a bond to yield-conscious investors is then countered by its increased attraction to capital gains-oriented investors.

☐ Size Of A Bond's Issue

Generally speaking, the smaller the size of a bond's issue, the higher will be its yield. This is primarily due to limited marketability of smaller bond issues to institutional investors. Most large instititions find holdings of less than 100 bonds ($100,000 worth) to be too small for efficient management. Many institutions may find less than 1000 bonds uneconomical.

Smaller bond issues which generate little institutional interest usually require a slightly higher coupon rate in order to be successfully marketed. Of course, this is to the advantage of individual investors. Bonds which may be lightly-traded should not be ignored by long-term investors.

☐ Nature Of the Bond Issuer's Business

It stands to reason that the safer a corporation's business is, the lower will be the interest rate on its bonds. Utility companies have always been considered relatively safe businesses, primarily because their services are often indispensible and they usually have a monopoly in the areas they serve.

In most states, public commissions (made up of political appointees) set utility rates. Utility corporations spend millions of promotional dollars to assure a friendly atmosphere before these commissions; consequently, it is unusual for any utility to operate unprofitably for even a single quarter. Exceptions have been some utilities located in large, poorly-managed cities during the mid-1970s and a few utilities with nuclear power problems in the late 1970s. Even these troubled utilities may sometimes warrant investor consideration though.

Extremely good yields and large capital gains were available to astute bond investors during the much-publicized Consolidated Edison/New York City problems in the mid-1970s. The following table provides prices at which various Consolidated Edision bonds could have been purchased during their "crisis" period and the prices 5 years later.

Bond Issue			Crisis Price	5 Years Later
ConEd 5%	1987	....	$420	$720
ConEd 7.9%	2001	....	480	810
ConEd 7¾%	2003	....	480	790
ConEd 9 1/8%	2004	....	540	930

Among other safe businesses are the drug industry and many of the food-related industries. Quality of management varies in all industries, so the bond investor should always take the time to adequately make comparisons.

Poor risk businesses include retail companies in the discount field and cyclical industries such as steel, automotive, and construction concerns.

*

PREDICABILITY OF INTEREST RATE TRENDS

Experienced persons understand both the importance of anticipating movements in interest rates *and* the difficulty in predicting these changes. An essential condition for understanding changing interest rate trends is accepting the fact that *long-term* predictions from any source are of limited value. Well-known economists who announce yearly predictions concerning the direction of interest rates normally are correct half of the time, and frequently less than that. Relative uncertainty in this area is often due to events which cannot be anticipated.

Nevertheless, investors should still attempt to anticipate *short-term* trends in interest rates. The first step in doing this is to know exactly where interest rates have been in the recent past (12 to 24 months). The second step is to be aware of current interest rate levels. By being well-informed in these areas, the bond investor will have a better opportunity to predict and benefit from changes in interest rate levels.

Perhaps, the more successful investor will keep in mind the following advice from Abraham Lincoln:

"The dogmas of the quiet past are inadequate to the stormy present. The occasion is piled high with difficulty, and we must rise with the occasion. As our case is new, so we must think anew and act anew, we must disentrall ourselves."

*

Chapter 4

WHERE ARE BONDS

AVAILABLE?

All stock brokerages can fill orders for listed bonds, however the availability of *new-issue* bonds often varies according to which brokerage group underwrites (markets) each new-issue.

Bond investors should always be cautious when opening an account at a brokerage, as most firms assign new customers to account executives on a "rotation basis." The persuasiveness and enthusiasm of some salespersons for non-bond investments may affect a bond investor's initial intentions. In addition, glowing research reports from brokerages often encourage the purchase of other items resulting in higher commissions.

In the search for a reliable account executive, sometimes it may be advisable to establish a brokerage account in another city when local assistance is insufficient. Many brokerages offer toll-free telephone lines for the convenience of distant customers.

*

BROKERAGE FIRMS

There are several types of brokerage firms. The most common is referred to as a "full-service" firm. There are also brokerages which specialize in particular areas, such as municipal bonds, options, or commodities. During the 1970s, another type of firm grew in popularity by offering deeply-discounted commissions.

☐ Full-Service Firms

These firms usually are members of large brokerage chains; and as their name implies, they offer a complete range of investment services. Their commissions vary somewhat, as does the quality of service provided. Research facilities and information are freely available and "Bond Guides" can usually be obtained by active bond customers. Advice is also available, often unsolicited.

Bond investors are more likely to locate specialists in bonds at full-service firms. These specialists will also handle orders in common stock investments, options, and possibly even commodities. Their advice in non-bond areas may be more realistic than that provided by ordinary account executives.

Commissions on bonds have increased considerably at full-service firms in the last 10 years. Whereas, the average bond commission was $5.00 per bond, it is now $7.50 to $10.00 per bond. Most firms have a minimum commission *per bond transaction* of $25.00 to $30.00, an amount necessary to cover basic costs. These minimum charges encourage the placement of orders which can be reasonably filled within a single day, which makes the availability of timely "Quote & Sizes" prior to entering orders a vital necessity.

☐ Discount Firms

Most discount firms offer deeply-discounted commissions to customers who require little research information or discussion concerning their investment ideas. Unless a bond investor has considerable experience and access to research information elsewhere, a discount firm's commission advantage may not outweigh other disadvantages.

Bond commissions at discount firms generally range from $3.00 to $4.00 per bond, with a minimum commission per transaction averaging approximately $30.00.

Services vary widely among discount firms. Some firms provide no research information at all, while others are willing to send almost everything to their clients that is available at full-service brokerages. "Traders" who field telephone calls from customers may restrict their conversations to order-taking only, which may or may not be desirable according to each individual investor's needs. Discount firms rarely employ anyone who is highly knowledgeable in the area of bonds.

As mentioned earlier, one of the most important services a bond investor requires is the availability of timely "Quote & Sizes" on bonds which are being considered for purchase or sale. At discount firms, this service may not be available at all; or if it is, some delay may be involved in obtaining it.

Another possible shortcoming at discount firms may be the lack of tax-free bonds as an investment medium. Unlisted taxable bonds also may be unavailable.

The following questions should be asked a discount firm prior to the opening of an account:

1. are timely "Quote & Sizes" available prior to placement of all orders,
2. what is the commission scale per bond,
3. what is the minimum commission on trades in the same security, in the same account, on the same day,
4. is research information provided on request, including "Bond Guides," and
5. are tax-free municipal bonds available?

☐ Municipal Bond Firms

Many firms located in the larger financial centers (New York City, Chicago, San Francisco, etc.) deal only in tax-free bonds. There are several reasons why some firms specialize in this field. Many municipal bond firms deal primarily with institutional customers, other brokerages, or very large individual investors.

Other firms may specialize in municipal bonds in order to serve relatively small buyers, primarily due to *extremely high commissions* which can be charged. Lack of a central marketplace or widely-advertised prices makes it very difficult for inexperienced buyers of municipal bonds to know the actual value of particular bond issues. Commissions in tax-free bonds are rarely printed on a customer's purchase or sale confirmation slip, therefore customers are often charged "whatever the traffic will bear."

Tax-free bonds listed for sale in offering sheets at *all* brokerages usually carry commissions of $20.00 to $30.00 per bond. Even $40.00 per bond is not unusual. Experienced tax-free bond buyers often have accounts at more than one firm (either full-service or municipal bond firms) in order to "double-check" prices which they are quoted. In dealing with a municipal bond salesperson (even a "bond expert"), a customer should not hesitate to openly discuss commission rates. Careful municipal bond buyers are often charged only $5.00 to $10.00 per bond, except on new-issues where underwriting brokerages set the commission rate.

The major disadvantage of dealing solely with a municipal bond firm is that the investor will not be made aware of attractive bonds in the *taxable* area. For many investors, taxable bonds may yield far more after taxes than a tax-free bond.

*

BUYING BONDS THROUGH BANKS

When an investor lives in a sparsely-populated area, a local bank may be the only source for bond investments. Fees at banks tend to differ according to the size of a customer's deposits.

Bond investors should be somewhat cautious in taking advice from local banks. Whereas, stockbrokers often offer advice which carries excessive risk, bank officers may provide advice which is too conservative. Most bank officers are experienced primarily in *short-term* U.S. Treasury and municipal securities due to the purchase requirements for bank assets. Bonds which are appropriate for a bank's short term liquidity requirements may not be suitable as long-term investments for individuals.

*

FEDERAL RESERVE BANKS & THEIR BRANCHES

Few investors realize that U.S. Treasury securities can be purchased directly from the Federal Reserve banks and their branches. During periods of high interest rates, obligations of the U.S. Treasury can offer both excellent yields and potential capital gains. During the late 1970s, interest rates on medium-term Treasury obligations often exceeded 9%.

Where possible, holders of U.S. Savings bonds (now yielding 6½ to 7%) should give serious consideration to switching such holding into the much higher rates offered by other government bond issues. The Federal Reserve does impose one limiting qualification for the purchase of most of their offerings — a $10,000 minimum purchase.

Potential buyers of U.S. Treasury bills (maturities of 1 year or less) are cautioned concerning limited liquidity of *direct purchases* from Federal Reserve banks. Certificates for Treasury bills are no longer issued, as ownership is accomplished by bookkeeping entries only. In order to liquidate such holdings prior to maturity, an owner must make their request by sending a certified or notarized letter to the Treasury Department in Washington, D.C. The Treasury Department then arranges for the transfer of the customer's account to a Federal Bank in the customer's area. This Federal bank then makes an entry for the account of the customer's commercial bank, through which the Treasury bills can finally be sold. These delays can be avoided by purchasing bills from a commercial bank.

The following list of Federal Reserve Banks and their branches can be utilized by interested persons to purchase high-yielding government bond issues.

Federal Reserve Bank Or Branch	Address
BOSTON	600 Atlantic Avenue Boston, Mas 02106 (617)973-3462
NEW YORK CITY	33 Liberty Street Federal Reserve PO Station New York, New York 10045 (212)791-5823

Buffalo — Branch   160 Delaware Avenue
PO Box 961
Buffalo, New York 14240
(716)849-5046

PHILADELPHIA   100 North Sixth Street
PO Box 90
Philadelphia, Penn 19105
(215)574-6580

CLEVELAND   1455 East Sixth Street
PO Box 6387
Cleveland, Ohio 44101
(216)241-2800

Cincinnati — Branch   150 East Fourth Street
PO Box 999
Cincinnati, Ohio 45201
(513)721-4787 ext. 333

Pittsburgh — Branch   717 Grant Street
PO Box 867
Pittsburgh, Penn 15230
(412)261-7864

RICHMOND   701 East Byrd Street
PO Box 27622
Richmond, Virginia 23261
(804)643-1250

Baltimore — Branch   114-120 East Lexington St.
PO Box 1378
Baltimore, Maryland 21203
(301)539-6552

Charlotte — Branch   401 South Tryon Street
PO Box 300
Charlotte, North Carolina
28230
(704)373-0200

ATLANTA   104 Marietta Street, NW
Atlanta, Georgia 30303
(404)586-8657

Birmingham — Branch   1801 Fifth Avenue, North
PO Box 10447
Birmingham, Alabama 35202
(205)252-3141 ext. 215

Jacksonville — Branch   515 Julia Street
Jacksonville, Florida 32231
(904)632-4245

Miami — Branch	3770 S.W. 8th Street
	Coral Gables, Florida 33134
	& PO Box 847
	Miami, Florida 33152
	(305)448-5732
Nashville — Branch	301 Eighth Avenue, North
	Nashville, Tennessee 37203
	(615)259-4006
New Orleans — Branch	525 St. Charles Avenue
	PO Box 61630
	New Orleans, Louisiana
	70161
	(504)586-1505 ext. 230, 240
CHICAGO	230 South LaSalle Street
	PO Box 834
	Chicago, Illinois 60690
	(312)786-1110
Detroit — Branch	160 Fort Street, West
	PO Box 1059
	Detroit, Michigan 48231
	(313)961-6880 ext. 372, 373
ST. LOUIS	411 Locust Street
	PO Box 442
	St. Louis, Missouri 63166
	(314)444-8444
Little Rock — Branch	325 West Capitol Avenue
	PO Box 1261
	Little Rock, Arkansas 72203
	(501)372-5451 ext. 270
Louisville — Branch	410 South Fifth Street
	PO Box 899
	Louisville, Kentucky 40201
	(502)587-7351 ext. 301
Memphis — Branch	200 North Main Street
	PO Box 407
	Memphis, Tennessee 38101
	(800)238-5293 ext. 225
MINNEAPOLIS	250 Marquette Avenue
	Minneapolis, Minnesota
	55480
	(612)340-2051

Helena — Branch	400 North Park Avenue Helena, Montana 59601 (406)442-3860
KANSAS CITY	925 Grand Avenue Federal Reserve Station Kansas City, Missouri 64198 (816)881-2783
Denver — Branch	1020 16th Street PO Box 5228, Terminal Annex Denver, Colorado 80217 (303)292-4020
Oklahoma City — Branch	226 Northwest Third Street PO Box 25129 Oklahoma City, Oklahoma 73125 (405)235-1721 ext. 182
Omaha — Branch	102 South 17th Street Omaha, Nebraska 68102 (402)341-3610 ext. 242
DALLAS	400 South Akard Street Station K Dallas, Texas 75222 (214)651-6177
El Paso — Branch	301 East Main Street PO Box 100 El Paso, Texas 79999 (915)544-4730 ext. 57
Houston — Branch	1701 San Jacinto Street PO Box 2578 Houston, Texas 77001 (713)659-4433 ext. 19, 74,75
San Antonio — Branch	126 East Nueva Street PO Box 1471 San Antonio, Texas 78295 (512)224-2141 ext. 61, 66
SAN FRANCISCO	400 Sansome Street PO Box 7702 San Francisco, California 94120 (415)392-6639

Los Angeles — Branch	409 W. Olympic Blvd
	PO Box 2077,
	Terminal Annex
	Los Angeles, California
	90051
	(213)683-8563
Portland — Branch	915 S.W. Stark Street
	PO Box 3436
	Portland, Oregon 97208
	(503)228-7584
Salt Lake City — Branch	120 South State Street
	PO Box 780
	Salt Lake City, Utah 84110
	(801)328-9611
Seattle — Branch	1015 Second Avenue
	PO Box 3567
	Seattle, Washington 98124
	(206)442-1650

In order to purchase U.S. Treasury securities, it is necessary to forward by mail or to personally deposit cash, a certified personal check, or a cashier's check at one of the listed banks with proper instructions. Detailed information concerning such purchases is provided by each bank upon request.

*

BOND MUTUAL FUNDS

Lacking adequate information in the past, many income-oriented persons have turned to bond mutual funds for additional income. A major factor encouraging the growth of bond mutual funds has been the 9 percent commission charged for their purchase, a source of considerable enthusiasm among brokerage salespersons. In the past, mutual fund buyers have often had a commission deducted from their initial investment capital which equalled or exceed *a full year's interest*. This excessive charge is still levied against many buyers of bond mutual funds; in many cases without the buyer's knowledge, as few persons would enter into such a transaction if they were well-informed.

Fortunately, there are now many bond funds which make no charge at all for mutual fund investments. These are called "no-load funds." Even without a commission charge however, the purchase of bond funds may not be advisable for many investors. If an investor has the time to read this book, they must also have time to plan their own bond investment program. The subject of bond mutual funds is thoroughly discussed in Chapter 12.

PART II

FINDING THE RIGHT BONDS

FOR YOUR NEEDS

Chapter 5

DOUBLING YOUR CAPITAL
IN BONDS

When most financial advisors suggest the possibility of doubling a client's capital, the degree of risk involved usually is far more than a prudent investor would assume. Most investors learn from experience that the greater the risk, the more likely one will lose instead of make money. Speculators who occasionally double their money usually have substantial tax-loss carryovers from previous investments to balance such gains.

There are basically three methods of using bonds to rapidly increase your capital:

1. tax-sheltered retirement accounts,
2. deeply-discounted bonds, and
3. convertible bonds,

These methods are discussed in the order of their safety and likelihood of success.

*

TAX-SHELTERED INVESTMENT ACCOUNTS

Everyone who holds securities and can qualify for a retirement account should have a portion of their assets in this form of tax-shelter. All self-employed individuals *or* employed persons without an employer-sponsored retirement plan can qualify for this type of investment account.

The main advantage of a retirement account is its total tax-free status during one's working years. Neither interest income nor capital gains are taxable *until* retirement. Another important inducement to establish these accounts is the tax deductibility of contributions.

☐ Contribution Limits

Contributions are limited in each taxable year, however considerable sums still can be deposited within a relatively short period of time. An unmarried employee, not having an employer-sponsored retirement plan, can establish an Individual Retirement Arrangement (IRA) in late December and contribute *as much as $4500* during the following 13 months. The maximum yearly contribution ($1500) can be made three times during this 13 month period:

1. $1500 in late December of year #1,
2. $1500 anytime during year #2, and
3. $1500 during early January of year #3.

A married person, with a non-working spouse, can contribute as much as $1750 per year to IRA plans, for a *total of $5250* over a 13 month period.

A married couple, each member qualifying for an IRA account, could contribute $4500 each during the 13 month period, for a *total of $9000*.

The self-employed person enjoys an even greater potential for obtaining tax deductions *and* sheltering income and capital gains. The maximum yearly contribution for a self-employed person to a Keogh Retirement Account is generally 15 percent of their income, up to $7500. This yearly amount, deposited three times during a 13 month period, would *total $22,500*. When contributions also are made for at least one employee of a self-employed person, an additional voluntary (non-deductible) contribution of 10 percent of income, up to $2500 yearly, can be made for the account of the self-employed person. This could elevate the 13 month contribution total *to $30,000*.

If a qualified investor already has long-term investments in stocks, bonds, or mutual funds, they should consider switching some of these assets into tax-sheltered retirement accounts the next time portfolio changes are contemplated. Should an emergency occur, funds can be withdrawn from such accounts. Withdrawals become reportable income in the year received, negating their previous tax deduction. A 10% withdrawal penalty is also assessed by the I.R.S., however this penalty may not be significant if the retirement account has existed for more than 2 years. This is due to the rapid growth of tax-free assets in such accounts.

☐ Time Required To Double Capital In Retirement Accounts

The following tables demonstrate the speed in which capital can double in retirement accounts. As bond interest is paid semi-annually, interest can be compounded every 6 months. The examples provided are at interest rate levels (10, 12, and 15%) which have prevailed in recent years.

The tables show the increase in capital from one's initial investment only; they do *not* include growth from additional yearly investments.

71

Table 1.   10% Compounded
            Interest On $10,000
            Investment

	Semi-Annual Interest	Cumulative Growth
6 mos.	$500	$10,500
1 yr.	525	11,025
1½ yr.	551	11,576
2 yr.	579	12,155
2½ yr.	608	12,763
3 yr.	638	13,401
3½ yr.	670	14,071
4 yr.	704	14,775
4½ yr.	739	15,514
5 yr.	776	16,290
5 ½ yr.	815	17,105
6 yr.	855	17,960
6 ½ yr.	898	18,858
7 yr.	943	19,801
7½ yr.	990	$ 20,791
8 yr.	1040	21,831
8½ yr.	1092	22,923
9 yr.	1146	24,069
9½ yr.	1203	25,272
10 yr.	1264	26,536
10½ yr.	1327	27,863
11 yr.	1393	29,256
11½ yr.	1463	$ 30,719

Table 2.   12% Compounded
            Interest On $10,000
            Investment

	Semi-Annual Interest	Cumulative Growth
6 mos.	$600	$10,600
1 yr.	636	11,236
1½ yr.	674	11,910
2 yr.	715	12,625
2½ yr.	758	13,383
3 yr.	803	14,186
3½ yr.	851	15,037
4 yr.	902	15,939
4½ yr.	956	16,895
5 yr.	1014	17,909
5½ yr.	1075	18,984
6 yr.	1139	$ 20,123
6½ yr.	1207	21,330
7 yr.	1280	22,610
7½ yr.	1357	23,967
8 yr.	1438	25,405
8½ yr.	1524	26,929
9 yr.	1616	28,545
9½ yr.	1713	$ 30,258

Table 3.   15% Compounded
            Interest On $10,000
            Investment

	Semi-Annual Interest	Cumulative Growth
6 mos.	$750	$10,750
1 yr.	806	11,556
1½ yr.	867	12,423
2 yr.	932	13,355
2½ yr.	1002	14,357
3 yr.	1077	15,434
3½ yr.	1158	16,592
4 yr.	1244	17,836
4½ yr.	1338	19,174
5 yr.	1438	$20,612
5½ yr.	1546	22,158
6 yr.	1662	23,820
6½ yr.	1786	25,606
7 yr.	1920	27,526
7½ yr	2064	29,590
8 yr.	2219	$ 31,809

☐ What Type Of Bonds Are Best For Retirement Accounts?

Bonds purchased for retirement accounts should be the highest yielding bonds available which provide adequate safety of principal. It is also important to choose new or recently-issued bonds which have no possibility of early redemption (within 5 to 10 years). If bonds chosen have similar interest payment dates, larger sums will be available more quickly for re-investment purposes. Larger re-investment sums allow a wider selection of bonds and may reduce commission costs.

Specific timing for bond purchases in a retirement account is not as crucial as for ordinary bond investments. Tax benefits from a retirement account are so beneficial that it seldom pays to delay purchase while hoping for slightly higher interest rates.

Price fluctuations are also less important, as the investor has little or no reason to actively buy or sell in a retirement account. If the initial interest rate is reasonably high, few other alternatives will justify the sale of such bonds. The longer the bonds are held, the sooner the capital can double and triple in value.

Bond mutual funds and money funds also can be used to establish retirement accounts; although, in the case of mutual funds, management fees and limited marketability problems reduce available yields somewhat. Chapter 15 provides additional details concerning the establishment of tax-sheltered retirement accounts.

*

DISCOUNTED BONDS

Discounted bonds, when held to maturity, have *built-in* capital gains. These are bonds which are selling substantially below par, usually because they have been issued during a prior period of much lower interest rates.

As the interest rate cycle progresses to higher yield levels, bonds issued in previous periods of lower rates must adjust downward in price to reflect the increasing coupon rates which are available in new-issue bonds. During these periods, excellent buying opportunities can be found in perfectly sound bonds which may be selling as much as $200 to $500 below par. At their maturity, or in many cases sooner if interest rates decline sufficiently, these bonds will appreciate back to their par value (or higher).

When purchasing discounted bonds, it's important to reasonably anticipate the future direction of general interest rates. The best time to purchase discounted bonds is just as interest rates peak and begin their downward cycle. Discounted bonds will be at their low at this particular time. Pinpointing such interest rate peaks is more of an art than a science.

☐ Useful Key To Identifying Interest Rate Peaks

Most of the time among similar-quality bond issues, long-term yields are higher than short-term yields. This is due to the greater risk involved during lengthier maturities. Nonetheless, there are short periods of time when this market condition is reversed: short-term rates actually *equal or exceed* long-term rates. This usually indicates that the general trend of interest rates will begin to decline, although such a decline may not begin immediately. In an exceptional case during the mid-1970s, the bond market did not turn until 15 months after this "signal" occurred. Abnormal factors (international events, government measures, and various shortages) contributed to this delay; as they may again do.

There are two basic "supply and demand" reasons why the temporary condition of *higher short-term* interest rates may exist:

1. during periods of high interest rates, many investors prefer longer maturity bonds in order to lock-in high interest rates and potential capital gains, and
2. most corporate and other borrowers, facing relatively high interest costs among all maturities in the bond market, may choose to incur necessary loans primarily on a short-term basis.

Greater demand for long-term bonds by investors and a *reduced supply* of these bonds from bond issuers naturally causes lower interest rates among longer maturities.

When an investor has funds available during interest rate peaks, it is not unusual to generate 20 to 30 percent capital gains within a few years time. Opportunities in discount bonds occur somewhat infrequently—on the average of once every 3 to 4 years.

76

□ Choosing Discounted Bonds

The deeper the discount below par of a bond, the greater will be its potential for capital gains. For this reason, investors often seek discount bonds selling between $500 to $800 when their primary goal is capital gains.

Current yields on discounted bonds are generally less than bonds selling close to par for two reasons:

1. their owners have the potential for capital gains in addition to earning a reasonable yield, and
2. due to the discounted price, owners have protection from early redemption by the bond issuer.

Experienced investors watch a list of 20 to 30 discount bonds on a regular basis, watching for oversold and overbought conditions. New investors should check the list of bonds trading daily in newspapers or "The Wall Street Journal." After compiling a list of possible investments, the next step is to determine the reason(s) for the bonds to be selling at discounted prices.

It's important to establish that the discount of a bond is due to conditions in the general bond market *and* not the result of financial problems of the bond issuer. When a particular bond issuer is experiencing financial problems, its bonds may fail to participate in a general bond rally. It's also prudent to avoid smaller bond issuers in *highly-cyclical* fields, as lower general interest rates usually are accompanied by business recessions. A lengthy recession may further weaken a cyclical corporation and keep its bonds from appreciating with other bonds.

*

CONVERTIBLE BONDS

A convertible bond can be exchanged for a specified number of shares of common stock at the option of the bondholder. In rare instances, a convertible bond can be exchanged for preferred stock or another bond.

A few terms should be reviewed:

conversion price: the figure which when divided into the bond's par value ($1000) determines the number of shares into which it is convertible.

conversion ratio: the number of shares into which the bond is convertible.

conversion value: the value of the bond if it were to be converted into common shares ("conversion ratio" times the market price of the common stock).

premium: the amount by which a convertible bond sells above its conversion value.

investment value: the value the bond would command in the open market if it were to sell on the basis of its yield, disregarding conversion privileges.

Conversion prices, quality ratings, and other data concerning convertible bonds are located in the back of the "Bond Guide."

The coupon rate of a new-issue convertible bond is usually one-third to one-half the yield of a comparable non-convertible bond, yet higher than the yield of the common stock into which it is convertible. The quality rating of most convertible bonds is one level below that of straight bonds of the same company, as convertible bonds are subordinate to these bonds.

In virtually all instances, convertible bonds sell at premiums above their conversion values. This is due to a number of factors, including:

1. a higher yield in comparison to its common stock,
2. in most cases, a reduced downside risk in comparison to its common stock,
3. buyer enthusiasm for such securities, and
4. the investment value of the bond.

In rare instances when a convertible bond falls below its conversion value, professional traders quickly take positions which eliminate such price differences.

☐ Why Are Convertible Bonds Issued?

An investor can better understand the risk of convertible bonds by learning why corporations issue such debt instruments. Normally, a corporation issues a convertible bond for one of two reasons, depending on its financial condition. By offering buyers a bond which is convertible into its common stock, a *financially-weak* corporation is often able to raise funds which might not be available otherwise. However attractive the convertible bonds of such a company may appear, their buyers have still acquired an investment in a business which the marketplace considers relatively insecure. This is not a good beginning for a prudent investment.

In other cases, a *strong* corporation may choose to use this form of financing to avoid paying a higher interest rate on straight bonds. These convertible bonds are usually in strong demand at their initial sale and often carry excessive premiums in the open market.

A review of convertible bond values in early 1980 revealed that only 15 percent of these bonds were selling above their initial issuance prices. The remaining 85 percent may have been issued by businesses in which most bond investors would rarely consider a common stock investment. In most cases the original owners of such bonds would have been better off to have acquired higher-yielding straight bonds of similar-quality issuers.

□ Why Buy Convertible Bonds?

Bond investors should *not* search financial pages of newspapers for bonds whose sole attraction is their convertibility. Buyers of high-priced (over $800) convertible bonds are required to choose correctly in *two areas,* the general direction of the stock market *and* the proper stock within this market. There is little reason for a bond investor to make the success of their investment program dependent on the bullishness of the stock market, in addition to assuming the inherent risk of individual stock holdings.

Another reason why these bonds may offer questionable value is the difficulty in determining the proper amount (premium) at which convertible bonds should sell over their conversion values. These premiums can range from 1 to 50 percent. When the premium is at the higher levels, an increase in the common stock's price may not necessarily lead to a similar increase in the price of the bonds. If a large premium exists on a discounted convertible bond, the investor must accurately assess the bond's *investment value.* On the other hand, when a large premium exists on a convertible bond selling above par, the investor must measure the degree of *other investor's enthusiasm* for the issue.

There are only a few reasons which justify the purchase of convertible bonds. When a stock investor intends to purchase a common stock, it is wise to check if the same company has a listed convertible bond available. As mentioned earlier, the comparatively higher yield of most convertible bonds can reduce one's downside risk somewhat. Commissions to acquire bonds are generally one-half the cost of purchasing a similar quantity of common stock also.

Another category of convertible bonds which investors might reasonably consider are those which are *deeply-discounted*. When a convertible bond is selling substantially below par, the primary influence on its price may be the movement of general interest rates rather than ordinary price changes of its common stock. In such cases, the investment value (or yield) of a convertible bond becomes increasingly important and may make certain of these bonds attractive investments for both capital gains and income. The major risk in buying such bonds is that their issuer may be having financial difficulties. The importance of carefully researching convertible bond alternatives cannot be overstressed.

☐ Redemption Of Convertible Bonds

How an investor should react to "notices of redemption" for convertible bonds varies considerably from that of non-convertible bonds.

When a convertible bond moves well *above par* in price, it is not unusual for the bond issuer to serve notice that they "intend to redeem" such bonds prior to normal maturity. This has the effect of *forcing bondholders* either to sell their bonds in the open market or to convert them into common stock. In such instances, an investor *should not* return their bond certificates to the bond issuer for redemption, as this might lead to unnecessary financial loss.

For example, let us assume we own a convertible bond which is selling for $1250 and we receive a notice of early redemption. Following such an announcement, the bond may adjust slightly in price to eliminate any existing premium (probably no more than $10 to $25 per bond.) We must then decide whether we wish to retain our investment in this company. If we do, then we simply instruct our brokerage to have the bonds converted into common stock, for which there is no fee. If we do not wish to retain the investment, we instruct the brokerage to sell the bonds at the highest price available.

The only circumstance in which a bondholder might permit such bonds to be redeemed at par by the issuer is if their price fell below par due to a rapid drop in the price of the common stock *after* the announcement of the redemption. This will seldom occur as the bond issuer would prefer to purchase their bonds in the open market if they suspected that the price of the bonds might fall *below par* at a time they wish to acquire their own bonds.

*

BUYING BONDS ON MARGIN

Borrowing to purchase additional bonds carries considerable risk, even more than margin-buying of common stock. With the same amount of capital, a speculator can purchase a greater *dollar amount* of bonds on margin than common stock. This greater margin simply increases the amount which can be lost if the speculator guesses wrong.

Margin buying also encourages emotional feelings, which do not contribute to intelligent decisions. Most bond investors should have little reason to consider margin purchases, as there are many other methods of obtaining excellent returns in bond investments which involve far less risk.

*

Chapter 6

Doubling Your Income In Bonds

In 1973, ordinary passbook accounts at savings and loan institutions in the United States contained more than $100 billion in individual savings. By 1978, these savings accounts had grown to more than $125 billion and were earning a taxable yield of 5¼% for their owners. During most of this 5-year period, these same individuals could have earned *double* the passbook interest rate by owning corporate bonds.

The type of bonds utilized to increase one's income depends on the specific needs of each investor. Two primary goals will be discussed:

1. more spendable income, and
2. more spendable tax-free income.

*

MORE SPENDABLE INCOME

Persons desiring more spendable income must seek taxable bonds paying the *highest coupon rate* with reasonable safety. For maximum income, the coupon rate or current yield of a bond is more important than its yield to maturity.

There are thousands of bonds available to investors desiring high income, however relatively few may prove suitable. This is because *callable* bonds with high coupon rates are usually among the first bonds to be redeemed during periods of low interest rates. Most listed bonds are callable.

□ Avoiding Callable Bonds

Bond issuers redeem bonds prior to maturity for several reasons, but primarily to re-finance bonded debt at lower interest rates *or* to retire bonds via a sinking fund. Bond holders who receive notices of redemption and wish to re-invest their funds may be forced to accept lower interest rates. To avoid this alternative, the intelligent investor can simply avoid callable bonds.

It is not possible to identify callable bonds by daily bond quotes which appear in financial sections of newspapers. However, this information does appear in the "Bond Guide," Standard & Poor reference books, on the back of bond certificates, and in final bond prospectuses.

In the "Bond Guide," redemption provisions are listed in the second section following each bond's description. As many as three different redemption prices may be listed:

1. the earliest *refunding* price and date,
2. the earliest sinking fund call price and date, and
3. the call price and date for *regular* redemptions.

Redemptions prices listed in the "Bond Guide" are the *current* call prices for each bond, as call prices frequently decline in amount each year.

The following examples taken from the "Bond Guide" may assist the reader in a better understanding of this important, but often ignored, subject:

| | —REDEMPTION PROVISIONS— | | |
	Refund Earliest Other	— Call Price — For S.F.	 Regular
Ford Motor Co. 9¼% 1994	[10]103.469	[11]100	±106.938
Pacific Telephone 9% 2018			[7]107.93
Southern Bell Tel. 8% 1999			±104.40

In the case of the Ford bond, $1034.69 is the current price at which the bond issue can be redeemed for *refunding purposes.* Its footnote '10' refers to July 15, 1984, which is the earliest date at which the bond can be redeemed for this purpose.

The next Ford call price, $1000.00, is the amount payable to bondholders if redemptions are made for *sinking fund purposes.* Its footnote '11' refers to July 15, 1979, the earliest date when such redemptions may commence.

The last Ford call price, $1069.38, is the current *regular* call price at which Ford may redeem all or part of this bond issue. The "plus & minus" symbol preceding this price reveals that this amount will decline during the following 12 months. As this "regular" call price has *no* numbered footnote, the Ford bonds are *immediately subject* to this redemption provision. A short review of the "Bond Guide" will reveal that most bonds have no numbered footnote preceding their call prices, which means that redemptions have already begun *or* may occur at anytime.

Bonds selling close to par which are subject to immediate call should be avoided *unless* a substantial premium over par is payable for such redemptions. For example, in the case of the Ford bond, the bond issuer must pay a premium of *$69.38 over par* per bond if they wish to redeem these bonds immediately via a "regular" call. It is somewhat unlikely that Ford or any other corporation would redeem recently-issued bonds at such a "regular" call premium, for several reasons:

1. if such bonds are a recent issue (the Ford bonds are 5 years old at this writing), the corporation has probably committed the proceeds of the bond issue into plant and equipment or whatever other financial use for which the funds were intended. If the corporation had sufficient excess funds to redeem a bond issue soon after its initial sale, they probably would not have sold the bond issue in the first place.

2. it would be poor corporate management to pay a substantial premium to redeem bonds soon after their initial issue. This premium penalty makes "regular" redemptions rare during the first few year of a bond's life.

In the case of the Pacific Telephone bond, the bond issue can be redeemed only by "regular" redemption at a price of $1079.30; however the footnote '7' reveals that these redemptions cannot take place until January 15, 1983. This bond issue was originally issued in 1978 and provides the standard 5-year call protection of most utility bonds.

The Southern Bell Telephone bond also has provision for only one call price, although in this case the bond issuer *currently* has the option to exercise a "regular" call at $1044.00. The symbol preceding the call price indicates that this amount will decline somewhat during the next 12 months. Redemption prices which begin at a premium approximating one year's worth of interest eventually decline to par or close to par.

An example of declining redemption prices are those for the Ford Motor Company 9.15% 2004 bonds:

Year	Percentage Of Principal Amount	Year	Percentage Of Principal Amount
1979	.... 108.00 %	1989	.... 102.50%
1980	...... 107.45	1990	...... 102.25
1981	...... 106.90	1991	...... 102.00
1982	...... 106.35	1992	...... 101.75
1983	...... 105.80	1993	...... 101.50
1984	...... 105.25	1994	...... 101.25
1985	...... 104.70	1995	...... 101.00
1986	...... 104.15	1996	...... 100.75
1987	...... 103.60	1997	...... 100.50
1988	...... 103.05	1998	...... 100.25

As discussed earlier, a few bond issuers have begun to set their initial redemption prices much lower than has been customary in the past. A brief example of this new trend is seen in the declining redemption prices of the Northwestern Bell Telephone 9½% 2016 bonds, which where issued in 1979. Although the Northwestern Bell Telephone bonds have a lower initial redemption price, their subsequent prices do not decline as quickly as prices in the Ford bond example.

Year	Percentage Of Principal Amount	Year	Percentage Of Principal Amount
1985	.... 104.75%	1992	.... 103.52%
1986	.... 104.57	1993	.... 103.34
1987	.... 104.40	1994	.... 103.17
1988	.... 104.22	1995	.... 102.99
1989	.... 104.05	1996	.... 102.81
1990	.... 103.87	1997	.... 102.64
1991	.... 103.69	1998	.... 102.46

If the letters 'NC' appear in the 'Regular' call column of a "Redemption Provisions" section, this means that the bond is not subject to redemption by this method.

Unless the bond investor has a "bond expert" for an account executive, they should not rely on their AE to interpret redemption provisions listed in the "Bond Guide." The bond investor should *personally* check this data when they have an opportunity to review a "Bond Guide" or other reliable sources. With the explanation provided above, this data is easily understood.

> *NOTE:* Bond investors should keep in mind that bond issuers will not necessarily redeem their bonds at the call prices listed in the "Bond Guide" or anywhere else. As discussed earlier, corporations will generally redeem their bonds by "open market" purchases when their bonds are selling *below par,* instead of paying bondholders intended call prices.

☐ Advantages Of New Bonds

Income-oriented investors should purchase either new-issue or recently-issued bonds in order to obtain bonds with maximum call protection. The purchase of a new-issue bond avoids the cost of a commission; however, careful investors should also review recently-issued bonds for possibly higher yields. During periods of high interest rates many corporations hesitate to issue long-term debt, which may significantly restrict choices and yields among new-issues compared to already-listed bonds.

Chapters 8 and 9 discuss opportunities and buying procedures for new-issue and listed bonds.

*

MORE TAX-FREE SPENDABLE INCOME

Many households now have two working adults. Even though "take-home" pay in such households may barely meet expenses, a joint tax bracket still can be quite high. When investment capital is placed into *taxable* bonds, much of the resulting income may be sacrificed to this high (or even higher) tax bracket.

In such homes, *tax-free yields* in local municipal bonds should be considered. Tax-free bonds generally yield *30 percent less* than similar quality taxable bonds. This means that households with tax brackets above 30 percent might obtain *more after-tax income* by owning municipal bonds.

When purchasing municipal bonds, it is equally important to avoid callable bonds. To obtain relevant data concerning tax-free bond call provisions, it is necessary to have a "bond expert" as one's account executive. Redemption provisions on municipal bonds are usually available only from municipal bond departments located in regional brokerage offices.

The purchase of new-issue municipal bonds provides the same call protection and commission advantages as described for taxable bonds. Further details concerning tax-free bonds appear in Chapter 12.

*

DIVERSIFYING YOUR PORTFOLIO

Investors in individual bonds should hold several different bond issues for:

1. greater safety, and
2. improved marketability.

How many different bonds should be owned by an investor depends on the amount of capital to be invested *and* whether taxable or tax-free bonds are being purchased.

☐ Taxable Bonds

When $5000 or less is available for investment, it is best to purchase high-quality bonds of just one issuer. With a $10,000 portfolio, *two* different bond issues should be held. An investor with $15,000 to $25,000 might purchase *3 to 4* different bonds. When the investable amount varies from $25,000 to $100,000, individual holdings might reasonably vary from *10 to 20 bonds each,* depending on investment opportunities. When more than $100,000 is available for investment, the investor may be required to consider tax-free bonds. If not, holdings might range from 25 to 50 bonds each.

The second reason for diversifying is to ensure that one's bonds can be quickly sold at a *fair market price*. Generally speaking in the *listed, taxable* bond market, the fewer bonds one holds in specific issues, the more quickly they can be sold at reasonable prices. For this reason, units of 5 to 10 bonds are preferred by many investors; however, commission costs at many brokerages encourages the ownership of 10 bond blocks instead of 5 bond holdings. Larger investors, for whom 10 bond blocks would be inconvenient, may require a day or two more to market their bonds at preferred price levels.

A minor benefit of diversification is the opportunity to purchase bonds with varying interest payment dates. This permits income to be more evenly-distributed throughout the year.

☐ Tax-Free Bonds

In the area of municipal bonds, marketability is often enhanced by *larger* positions due to institutional demand. While the tax-free bond investor may wish to diversify somewhat for greater safety, the size of individual holdings should not be less than 10 bonds. Smaller holdings often suffer a price penalty ($5.00 to $10.00 per bond) when they must be sold.

When capital permits, units of 25, 50, or 100 bonds should be purchased, as these sizes are more readily marketed and may command slightly higher prices ($2.50 to $5.00 per bond). Marketability and buying procedures for municipal bonds are discussed in greater detail in Chapter 12.

*

Chapter 7

Doing Your Bond Research

"Interest rates are going down. I think the long-term rates on bonds could go down to 6%, maybe 5% in a couple of years."

....Robert S. Driscoll, President
Lord, Abbet & Company (July 1, 1977)

The above statement by Mr. Driscoll is from a source which may be more interested in marketing bond securities than conducting serious bond research. Lord, Abbet & Company is one of the largest management firms of bond mutual funds in the United States. *One year after* this public statement appeared in "Forbes Magazine," bond interest rates were ranging between 9% and 11%. Investors must be cautious in reviewing material from sources within the securities industry, as much of this information may exhibit a conflict of interest.

*

RESEARCHING A SPECIFIC BOND

Intelligent investors should consider the following research sources in the order listed:

1. bond offerings listed in "The Wall Street Journal" and brokerage listings,
2. bond issuer data in the "Bond Guide,"
3. bond issuer data in the "Stock Guide,"
4. the Standard & Poor's sheet of the bond issuer and/or prospectus of a new-issue,
5. Standard & Poor's or Moody's reference volumes, and
6. the bond issuer's quarterly and annual reports.

☐ List Of Available Bonds

Locating bonds which are available for investment is easily done. In larger cities, the local newspaper probably lists daily trading activity in bonds on the major exchanges.

When a local newspaper does not provide bond quotes, then the investor should go to their public library and locate recent issues of "The Wall Street Journal." This publication lists all trading activity in listed bonds; and in addition, it has a special page devoted to news of the bond market.

A third source of available bonds are "offering sheets" distributed by brokerages. Most brokerage firms provide periodic (often weekly) lists of bonds which are available for sale to their clients. The same offering sheet may provide separate lists for new-issue bonds and those bonds which have already been issued. The prices on already-issued bonds may or may not reflect "fair market prices." It is important for investors to compare prices on these sheets before making investment decisions.

☐ "Bond Guides" and "Stock Guides"

A one-minute review of a "Bond Guide" can provide the following basic information:

1. the type of bond involved,
2. its interest payment dates and precise maturity date,
3. its quality rating,
4. a 3-year record of the bond issuer's "interest charges versus earnings" ratio,

90

5. redemption provisions,
6. size of the bond's issue, plus total long-term debt,
7. price trading ranges of the bond, and
8. recent current yield *and* yield to maturity figures for the bond.

The "Bond Guide" provides this information for more than 4800 straight bonds and limited data on more than 600 convertible bonds. Obtaining a copy of a recent "Bond Guide" can pose a problem for occasional bond buyers. One way to obtain a "Bond Guide" is to contact an office manager of a brokerage and specifically request the services of a salesperson who specializes in bonds. When such a salesperson is available, they may be able to furnish a relatively recent copy to a potential customer.

"Bond Guides" can also be purchased directly from their publisher:

Parts Department
Standard & Poor's Corporation
25 Broadway
New York, New York 10004

As the current price ($7.75) for a single "Bond Guide" is subject to change, interested persons should enclose at least a dollar extra to cover price increases, postage, and handling charges.

If the quality rating, interest payment dates, or any other provisions of a bond prove unattractive, this can be determined in a short time with a "Bond Guide." On the other hand, if this preliminary data appears satisfactory, the next step is to review bond issuer data in the "Stock Guide," which is also published by Standard & Poor's Corporation (base price: $5.75). "Stock Guides" are readily available in most brokerage offices.

Although an indication of a bond issuer's profitability appears in the "Bond Guide," more detailed information is available in the "Stock Guide." Relevant data in the "Stock Guide" includes:

1. the principal business of the bond issuer,
2. the number of years in which consecutive dividends have been paid, and most important,

3. the earnings record of the bond issuer for the last 4 to 5 years.

The nature of a bond issuer's business, their ability to earn consistent profits, and the payment of regular dividends are among the most important indications of an ability *to pay scheduled interest on bonds* and *to retire bonds at their maturity.* Bonds of a company with widely fluctuating profits and a poor (or non-existent) dividend record are often an unreasonable risk for prudent bond investors. However, if profits are steadily growing or are maintained at a high level and dividends have been paid regularly for a number of years (10 or more), then the next step is an even closer review of the bond issuer's financial record.

□ S&P Sheet or Prospectus

While many experienced investors might have both a "Bond Guide" and "Stock Guide" in their possession already, the next research source will involve either a phone call or trip to a brokerage office. This research source is the latest individual data sheet on the bond issuer, the most commonly-available being those published by Standard & Poor's Corporation (often referred to as "S&P" sheets).

These, or similar data sheets from another publisher, can be obtained at almost all brokerage offices, usually at no charge. They are normally updated every three months after each quarter's earnings are announced, or more often in the case of major corporate developments.

The front of the S&P sheet describes recent (within the last 12 months) financial progress of the bond issuer, with very general predictions of future profitability. Quarterly sales and earnings figures are provided, which are often the best indications of profitability in the near term. The reverse side of the S&P sheet provides a 10-year record of sales, profits, dividends, and related financial data. It also describes the nature of the firm's business in detail. This information is important, as it can indicate past problems which may re-occur.

It is essential to look for profit levels which have *always* permitted the payment of interest on bonds. Increasing profits each year are not as vital as a consistent level of profitability. The S&P sheet can reveal this status at a glance.

These sheets should be obtained and reviewed *prior* to any investment.

When a potential bond investment is a *new-issue,* regulations of the Securities And Exchange Commission permit brokerages to furnish only a "preliminary prospectus" to customers. These booklets are published by the bond issuer or their brokerage underwriting group. They can range from 15 to 60 pages in length, describing a company's financial history in great detail.

Supposedly, a prospectus reveals all of the most up-to-date developments within a corporation which intends to issue new bonds or stock. However, some companies may prefer to be less candid than others, so the accuracy and completeness of data provided in these booklets can vary. A prospectus usually makes for very ponderous reading, as they are compiled for the most part in the language of attorneys.

If an investor is interested in a new-issue bond and does not wish to devote the necessary time to decipher information contained in a preliminary prospectus, they should request a copy of the bond's S&P sheet by telling an account executive that they're "interested in investing in the common stock of the company." This should permit the brokerage to provide a S&P sheet. When a brokerage office is within close proximity, the investor can simply walk into the office and request the S&P sheet.

☐ Reference Books & Corporate Reports

The final step in researching bonds may be to check the large reference volumes found in most brokerages. These financial references are in encyclopedic form and provide the most detailed information on past bond issues and their issuers. Specific redemption terms can be determined in these references as well as details concerning the structure of each corporation.

Quite often, these books contain more up-to-date information than is provided by S&P sheets, as they are updated on a daily basis. These references are published by several research firms, but again the Standard & Poor's reference books seem to be the most-widely distributed.

Occasionally, a brokerage office also will have a file containing recent annual and quarterly reports of bond issuers. When available, these reports are worth checking too.

☐ Bond Advisory Services

There are several bond advisory services which frequently advertise in financial magazines and business sections of major newspapers. These services may be most useful when they provide a general review of known facts as they relate to individual bonds. Recommendations by these services often cause price reactions in favored bonds before their average subscribers can react. Their predictions concerning interest rate trends are generally more reliable than those from brokerage sources, as many brokerages tend to present a "positive" view even when they know they should not.

For most investors, the expense of these advisory services may not be justified unless large (over $100,000) portfolios are being managed. Investors who will devote the *necessary* time can review most of the same research information which is available to these services.

*

RESEARCHING THE GENERAL BOND MARKET

Continuous review of overall conditions in the bond market provides the investor with an improved indication of future interest rates and also attractive opportunities in individual bonds. While the assistance of a "bond expert" can prove invaluable, a fair number of bond investors may be unable to locate such professional assistance. These investors will find reliable sources of general information in the following publications:

1. "The Wall Street Journal,"
2. "Barron's,"
3. financial sections of large newspapers, and
4. a few financial magazines.

☐ "The Wall Street Journal"

One page of each issue of this publication is devoted to a review of developments in the new-issue bond market. Quite often, more than a billion dollars worth of new bonds, both taxable and tax-free, are issued in a week. How these new-issues fare among bond buyers should be of interest to anyone who is considering the purchase *or* sale of bonds.

When a new-issue is quickly sold-out on the first day it is available, this may indicate:

1. the bond's yield was considered attractive compared to other available bonds,
2. debt of the bond issuer was in exceptional demand due to scarcity of other issues,
3. the commission paid to salespersons recommending the bond was above-average, and/or
4. the general level of interest rates is expected to either decline or remain stable.

Of course, when new-issue bonds do not sell quickly, the opposite conclusions might be drawn. By reading the 'Bond Markets' page of "The Wall Street Journal," a bond investor frequently can determine the specific reason for a new-issue's success or lack of success. Over a period of a few months, this overall knowledge may provide an improved understanding of current interest rate trends.

This publication occasionally prints lengthy articles on new developments within the bond market, normally on the same page that new-issues are discussed. Advantages and disadvantages of new bond products are usually outlined impartially, except for quotes from industry sources. Quite often, this reporting style leaves the reader with a neutral impression, which may be fortunate in the case of many investment options promoted by the brokerage industry.

"The Wall Street Journal" is published Monday through Friday and can be subscribed to by writing:

The Wall Street Journal
200 Burnett Road
Chicopee, MASS 01021

Its yearly cost is currently $55. Most libraries subscribe to this publication.

□ "Barron's"
"Barron's" is a weekly financial newspaper published primarily for those within the securities industry. Its weekly column on bonds, usually under 'Capital Markets,' often provides more detailed explanations for the successes and failures among new-issues than is available in "The Wall Street Journal." An example appeared in the June 18, 1979 issue:

"Nortek's 20-year debentures undoubtedly will be peddled aggressively, as they reward brokerage salesmen with a fat commission of about $32.50 for each $1000 face amount rather than the standard fee of $20 to $25."

The low-rated ('B') Nortek 12½% 1999 bonds were issued during a period of unusually high interest rates.

"Barron's" should be periodically reviewed to gain a more thorough knowledge of the bond markets. A yearly subscription currently costs $36 and can be obtained at the same address as "The Wall Street Journal." Most libraries subscribe to this publication also.

☐ Business Sections Of Newspapers

Other than bond quotes, most newspapers offer little information to readers on the subject of bonds. Numerous papers in large cities do not even provide a complete list of bond quotes. However, business sections of newspapers should still be reviewed for announcements of changes in the prime rate and other well-known interest rates. On Tuesdays, the yield figures for new U.S. Treasury offerings should be noted. Changes in these rates often foretell new directions in other interest rates.

Business sections of newspapers also are a source of advertisements for various types of "no-load" mutual funds (those which do not charge an acquisition fee). Since these mutual funds are not marketed through brokerages, they must rely on advertising to reach their potential investors. Readers should realize that few newspapers or magazines exercise control over the reliability of their advertisements. The reader must exercise this caution, remembering that attractive investment opportunities seldom require extensive advertising or other promotion.

☐ Financial Magazines

With few exceptions, financial magazines rarely display concern for the bond market. The "periodical guides" in libraries should be used to locate infrequent bond articles in these magazines.

Only "Forbes" provides a regular review on bonds. This one-page review is unique in that its author, Ben Weberman, is generally willing to express opinions and predictions concerning future interest rates. However, his candor and reserve in expressing such predictions appeared in his article of January 22, 1979:

> "The forecasters are evenly divided — and almost all are without deep conviction. As my readers know, I am not normally a fence sitter. I usually put my neck out, sometimes with fortunate results, as in 1975-77; sometimes with terrible results, as last year. But this time I am genuinely perplexed."

Articles which do appear in financial magazines concerning bonds are usually the result of current public interest in a particular bond vehicle, many of which are discussed in Chapter 13.

*

BROKERAGE RESEARCH & OTHER UNRELIABLE SOURCES

Brokerages are ready sources of facts pertaining to individual bond issues, but poor sources for predictions of future interest rates. Brokerages depend upon the income generated from sales of both listed and unlisted securities. Most of their unlisted bond sales are new-issues. As it is important for a brokerage to market new-issue bonds whether yields are high or low, they normally refrain from recommending investor caution during a period of rapidly rising interest rates.

Many firms also prefer to recommend security investments which result in higher commissions. At most brokerages, listed bond commissions are among the lowest fees as a percent of the capital being committed. Bonds which are recommended by a brokerage will normally be the higher commission new-issues or bond mutual funds.

The size of a brokerage's inventory can also influence their stance toward bond investments. Brokerages with large bond inventories tend to take bullish stances in their public comments; whereas, the opposite opinion might be expressed by a brokerage with a low inventory.

In addition, many brokerages are strongly influenced by the investment desires of principal customers such as institutions. Individual investors are often considered convenient outlets for holdings which large institutional customers wish to dispose of quickly at favorable prices. Consequently, brokerage research reports, newsletters, and other public announcements are often colored by these "conflicts of interest."

☐ Bankers

Most bank employees who deal with the public have very little training in any area of securities. Their knowledge of bonds may even be less than that of the average stockbroker. Those bankers having some knowledge of bonds are often limited in their experience to those securities which banks normally own, which are usually government bonds having relatively short maturities. Bank-oriented investments may be suitable for some individuals on a short-term basis; however, on a longer term basis, the majority of investors can earn far more income in lengthier maturities.

Perhaps the best source of information on changing bond markets is *the well-informed investor*. The few reliable publications discussed in this chapter will provide interested individuals an excellent start toward this goal.

*

Chapter 8

Buying New-Issue Bonds

Investors often receive phone calls from their brokerages offering "new-issue" bonds. This term is used to describe the original sale of bonds. Account executives often emphasize that new-issue bonds can be purchased without having to pay a commission. Since many investors relish buying a "bargain," these new-issues may sound quite attractive. However, each new-issue offering must be judged on its own merits, as this bond source may offer both bargains and poor values.

*

BENEFITS OF BUYING NEW-ISSUE BONDS

There are several distinct advantages to buying bonds during their original issue, providing the terms of such bonds compare favorably with bonds which are already issued and listed.

☐ No Acquisition Fee

While it is true that no commission is charged the buyer of a new-issue, there is still a commission in the overall transaction. The bond issuer is charged this commission, which often exceeds normal bond commission rates. The amount of this charge varies with the quality of the bond and the general difficulty in marketing bonds at the time the bond is issued. The lower the quality of the bond *and* the more difficult to issue bonds in general, the higher the commission will be.

The new-issue commission on the average *taxable* bond in a normal market ranges from $5.00 to $10.00 per bond. A lower-quality taxable bond in a difficult bond market may have a commission ranging from $15.00 to $35.00 per bond. When the commission is this high, many AEs are willing to work longer hours to inform their clients of such "opportunities." Few customers will realize when an AE is so motivated, as new-issue commissions are not divulged on purchase confirmation slips. An example of how commissions can affect new bond issues was described in the "Barron's" weekly bond column of March 5, 1979:

> "Oversupply jitters also arose in the tax-exempt sector on Tuesday when an icy reception was accorded to $125 million of Connecticut bonds priced to yield between 5.4% in 1980 and 6.05% in 1999. Only $55 million of the double-A securities were retailed that day. Eventually, however, the remainder moved briskly owing to a determined effort by salesmen who had been offered an increased commission fee for soliciting orders."

Another example appeared in "The Wall Street Journal" on April 27, 1979:

> "Bond salesmen were inspired by a sizeable $11 credit for every $1,000 of new Louisiana Power & Light Co. bonds they could retail. Thus, in the face of a very weak market for older utility bonds, this $45 million issue was said to be 75% placed by last night.

Most new-issue commissions are not revealed until other bond terms are announced on the date of sale. However, when a bond is expected to be particularly difficult to market, the commission may be set quite high and will be announced several days prior to the sale date in order to motivate salespersons.

The commission on new *tax-free* bonds is normally higher than those for taxable issues. Most new tax-free bonds which are commonly sold to individual investors have a commission of $10.00 to $20.00 per bond. In some markets, these commissions may range as high as $30.00 to $40.00 per bond.

A period in which commissions begin to increase for new-issues often indicates that generally higher interest rates are expected. The highest commissions usually occur when interest rates peak — the best time to be purchasing long-term bonds. A high commission should not be a deterent to the purchase of a new-issue, providing the bond's quality level is within preferable limits.

On *taxable* new-issues, the final prospectus will provide an approximation of a bond's commission. This information appears on the front of the prospectus. An example are the terms which appeared on the final prospectus of the Pacific Telephone & Telegraph 9.75% 2019 bonds issued in 1979:

	Price To Public	Underwriting Discounts	Proceeds To Company
Per Debenture	100.00%	.875%	99.125%
Total	$300,000,000	$2,625,000	$297,375,000

The "underwriting discount" of .875% is the equivalent of $8.75 per bond. In this example, the actual gross commission to AEs might be somewhat less than $8.75, possibly $6.50 to $8.00. The net commission earned by the AE ranges from 35 to 50 percent of the gross commission. Tax-free bond issuers do not issue a prospectus which can be made available to the public, therefore the commissions on their new-issues can be determined only by direct inquiry to an AE.

☐ Little Or No Accrued Interest

Most investors wish to avoid accrued interest during the purchase of bonds. Until accrued interest is returned at the next interest payment date, it represents an extra charge to the bond buyer.

New bonds are issued with little or no accrued interest. As discussed earlier, virtually all interest payment dates are scheduled on either the *first or fifteenth* of the month. How much interest appears on the purchase confirmation of new-issue bonds depends on how many days separate the sales date of the new-issue from the bond's nearest interest payment date. Usually any accrued interest on new-issues is less than $4.50 per bond.

☐ Available At Or Near Par

Many investors prefer to purchase bonds at or near par in order to make their investments in increments of $1000 each. All new-issue taxable bonds are marketed at par or within a few dollars per bond of this figure. Most tax-free bonds which mature in more than 15 years are also issued at or close to par.

☐ Possibility Of Quick Premium

Favored customers at brokerages may be told of new bonds which are expected to go to a premium immediately upon their issue. This premium seldom amounts to more than $5.00 to $15.00 per bond, depending on the scarcity of the new-issue and the strength of public and institutional demand. In the past, such premiums often occurred with the issuance of convertible bonds.

These premiums are occasionally available now during the issue of bond "units," in which each bond is sold with a specified number of common shares. The stock is offered as an inducement to bond buyers, who hope that the quantity of stock offered, plus the bond's coupon rate will cause the total value of the unit to quickly exceed its original cost. Sometimes, these unit offerings result in premiums; sometimes they do not. Premiums which do result may be partially offset by the eventual commission to dispose of relatively small amounts of unwanted common stock.

On rare occasions, a "bond expert" may recognize a new-issue as potentially underpriced by its underwriting syndicate. This circumstance may occur for a variety of reasons, but primarily due to general ignorance by investors of the intrinsic value of a new-issue. It is not unknown for the underwriting syndicate to err also. Persons controlling these offerings, both at the bond issuer level and within managements of brokerages, often are better experts at marketing bonds than analyzing them.

*

PROBLEMS WITH NEW-ISSUES

Perhaps the greatest problem posed by new-issue bonds is the "last minute" announcement of their terms. A listed bond can be watched for days or weeks while a decision is pondered, while in the case of an attractive new-issue the decision may have to be made in a matter of hours or even minutes after the bond's terms are announced.

Whichever day a new-issue is scheduled to be sold, its final terms normally are announced *no sooner* than the previous day (and then only after the close of the New York Stock Exchange — 4 PM Eastern Standard Time).

When clients are difficult to reach, their AEs may not be able to contact them until the day of the new-issue's sale. If bonds are still available the day of their sale, there may be little time to make a decision before the issue is sold-out. How quickly a new bond will sell-out depends on how favorable its terms are and the general bond market. Some new issues in a favorable bond market are sold-out weeks *ahead* of their sales date, while others cannot be completely marketed without a downward price adjustment (discussed later in the chapter).

Most brokerages attempt to gauge the possible terms of new-issues well before their sale and thereby provide their AEs with close estimates of expected terms. Customers can then *reserve* bonds on the basis of these estimates. This procedure is fully described at the end of the chapter.

□ Minimum Purchase Orders

The minimum size of new-issue purchase orders for both taxable and tax-free bonds is usually 5 bonds or $5000 worth of the issue. When more than 5 bonds are desired, customers may be encouraged to purchase in increments of 5 bonds (10, 15, etc.)

Some firms permit smaller investors to pool their funds in order to meet minimum order sizes. After the purchase is accomplished in one account, delivery instructions can be given the brokerage to split the 5 bonds accordingly. Customers must arrange such pooling on their own, which may be preferred in any case. No additional fees should be necessary as long as delivery instructions are sent to the brokerage soon after the purchase.

☐ Selection Limited

The number of new-issues marketed each week varies greatly. In any one week, the number of new bonds suitable for a particular investor's need may number anywhere from none to more than ten. When relatively few bonds are being issued, bond buyers may have to postpone investing for several weeks until an acceptable new-issue appears. In order to locate a reasonable yield, many investors turn to listed bonds during periods of little new-issue activity.

☐ Poor Marketability Until Listed

After a new-issue is sold, the corporate bond issuer must submit a listing application to an exchange if they wish to have their bonds listed. The processing of this application may require a month or more. Meanwhile, the bond will trade in the over-the-counter market. If an owner must sell their new bonds prior to their being listed, the sales price in the o-t-c market may not be as favorable as when the bond is listed.

Another limitation during the interim before listing is that such bonds have no loan value. If the investor had purchased listed bonds instead, a loan of 50 percent or more of the bond's value could be obtained — which might avoid the need for selling in some cases.

☐ Overbidding And Overpricing

The investor who relies solely on new-issues as a source of bond purchases *without* adequate research may not always purchase good value.

Bond issuers and brokerage underwriting groups arrive at terms for new-issues by one of two methods:

1. a brokerage or brokerage group and the bond issuer set the terms which other brokerages must accept if they wish to participate in the bond's marketing, or
2. various brokerage groups participate in an "auction" by submitting sealed bids to the bond issuer. The group offering the least cost (lowest bond yield) to the bond issuer wins the bidding.

During periods of slackened new-issue activity, brokerages may overbid (offer too low a cost to the bond issuer) in their efforts to obtain this lucrative business. As a result of offering too favorable terms to the bond issuer, the winning brokerage group may offer *less than favorable* terms to investors. This may cause serious problems in marketing such bonds; and frequently, it is not possible to sell the entire bond issue at its original terms. The remaining unsold portion of the new-issue is then "released from marketing restrictions" and permitted to decline to a price which is generally acceptable to investors. Individuals who have already purchased the new-issue at its original price may be somewhat unhappy with this result, *if* they are aware of it. These price "adjustments" are reported in "The Wall Street Journal" on a regular basis:

February 23, 1979 ..... "Georgia Power Co.'s new 10½% bonds plunged the equivalent of about $22.50 for every $1000 face amount from their original price of 100 set just one day earlier. The Southern Co. unit's $100 million offering had attracted scant initial demand. Yesterday therefore, the many unsold bonds were tossed onto the resale market at a substantially lower price of about 97½ bid, 97¾ asked."

July 25, 1979 .... "Public Service Electric and Gas Co.'s 9.75% bonds tumbled about $10 for every $1000 face amount when freed to trade in the secondary market yesterday. At the adjusted price, the 30-year bonds yield close to 9.8%. The $100 million issue reached investors initially last week at a 9.72% yield."

Prior to committing funds to new-issue bonds, the investor should be reasonably well-informed of comparable yields of other new-issue bonds and also listed bonds.

*

HOW TO BUY NEW-ISSUES

It is vital for investors to have a reliable source of information on upcoming new-issues. Without reasonably accurate estimates of expected terms, a customer has little basis to make reservations for new-issue bonds. The best source of this information is an account executive who:

1. works for a brokerage which keeps salespersons well-informed, and also
2. specializes in bond investments.

Finding such an AE is the subject of a later chapter. Locating a brokerage which keeps salespersons informed in this area may involve a trial-and-error process.

□ Know The State Of The Bond Market

In some new-issue markets, yields of new bonds may actually be *below* listed yields of comparable quality. This disparity often stems from strong institutional demand, which is more readily satisfied by the new-issue market where a large buyer can purchase in volume at will. In such markets, the individual investor may find that new bond yields are too low compared with listed yields (even after commission charges for listed bonds).

The new-issue investor should also stay aware of *previous* new-issue yields. By knowing the yields available during the previous few weeks, one can better judge the attractiveness of current bond offerings.

□ Make Sure The Bond Will Be Listed

When buying a new-issue bond, always assure that the bond issuer intends to apply for the bond's listing. At this time, only half of all outstanding bond issues listed in the "Bond Guide" are listed on an exchange. The unlisted bonds have no collateral value. They also have relatively poor marketability compared to listed bonds when the investor wishes to sell.

□ Obtaining The Preliminary Prospectus

When notified of an interesting new-issue, the investor may wish to request a copy of the bond's preliminary prospectus. This booklet describes the issuer's financial background in great detail, in addition to describing the particular type of bond to be issued. The terms of the bond *do not* appear in the preliminary prospectus (blank spaces are left in place of the terms.).

A frequent buyer of new-issues may become accustomed to their weighty style and actually prefer these booklets to the S&P sheet of the bond issuer. However, some brokerages may not be able to furnish a preliminary prospectus on a timely basis. In such cases, the bond issuer's S&P sheet should be requested in the manner described in the previous chapter.

□ Make Reservations As Early As Possible

Once an investor has an opportunity to review research data on a new-issue and decides to make a purchase, a "reservation" should be placed for the bonds. This reservation should be made as early as possible, as attractive new-issues are usually sold on a first-come-first-served basis.

Such reservations should always be *conditional*. If the AE quotes an expected yield figure which is satisfactory to the investor, then the reservation should be made on the basis of the quoted yield, or within specified limits of this figure. When making reservations, it is customary to provide some leeway (1/8 to 1/4 of a percentage point) from the expected yield figure. Minimum acceptable yield figures should be discussed in detail with the AE.

When the announced terms are within acceptable limits, there should be no need for the AE to re-contact the investor. The reservation can automatically become an order. As it may be difficult to reach a large number of customers on busy days, the AE will appreciate the time saved by not having to make unnecessary telephone calls. Of course, if the announced terms are less than have been stipulated in one's reservation, then the AE must call the investor to discuss whether any new circumstances warrant consideration of the lower yield.

A number of guidelines are suggested for investors who frequently purchase new-issue bonds:

1. reserve the maximum number of bonds you might wish to purchase, as it is easier to reduce the size of an order than to increase it. The AE should be told if you are reserving more than you may take. Most AEs will cooperate when their firm permits.
2. reserve issues that you genuinely intend to purchase if the terms meet your requirements, otherwise your AE may hesitate to accept future reservations,
3. immediately notify your AE if you wish to alter or cancel a reservation, and

4. purchase all of your new-issues from the *same* AE. New-issue prices are the same at all firms (except for some taxable bonds). By concentrating these purchases where the service is best, you may receive favored treatment when especially attractive new-issues become available.

*

Chapter 9

Buying Listed Bonds

Most listed bonds (approximately 93 percent) appear on the New York Stock Exchange. The balance are listed on the American Stock Exchange and a few regional exchanges.

Listed bonds are always taxable bonds, generally issued by business corporations. Most large corporations choose to list their bonds in order to enhance the marketability of their new-issues and thereby obtain a slightly lower coupon rate compared to similar quality bonds for which no listing is planned.

With few exceptions, neither taxable nor tax-free bonds issued by various local, state, federal, or related agencies are listed. There is no reason why the larger government bond issues could not be listed, except it has not been the custom to do so. Government bonds would certainly be more popular investments if they were listed, which might even result in lowered interest costs for such issuers.

*

ADVANTAGES OF LISTED BONDS

The most important advantage of purchasing listed bonds is improved marketability. Wider selectivity, no minimum order size, and collateral value are other significant advantages.

☐ **Improved Marketability**

Most investors in taxable bonds prefer to choose from those bonds which are listed or for which listing is intended. A bond which is listed permits its owner to easily keep track of its value and potential selling price. Most brokerage offices can instantly furnish a reliable "Quote & Size" on listed bonds using electronic quote machines. Obtaining similar quotes on unlisted bonds may or may not be possible, depending on the brokerage office.

Unlisted bond quotes from different firms may vary widely, often by as much as $30.00 to $40.00 per bond. When the sellers of o-t-c bonds contact only one firm for a quote, their bonds may be sold for far less than might be available elsewhere.

☐ **Wider Selection**

There are more than 2500 bonds listed for trading on the New York Stock Exchange and the American Stock Exchange. The number of new-issue bonds which become available each month generally varies from 20 to 40 issues, and only a few of these may be suitable for a particular individual's needs.

Approximately 900 different bonds trade on a daily basis on the above exchanges. Many widely-held bonds trade everyday, while other issues may trade only once or twice a week. An average of 1700 different bonds trade at least once a week, consequently bond buyers should utilize the *weekly* bond listings (which appear on Sundays in most major newspapers) when searching for potential bond investments.

This wide variety allows investors to choose from many bonds in almost any category. If an income-oriented investor wishes to own an 'A' rated industrial bond maturing in 20 years and selling at least 10 percent below par, there may be 40 to 50 different choices each day in the listed bond markets. If one's first investment choice proves difficult to purchase at a reasonable price, there are many other choices which may be equally attractive and easier to buy.

When daily volume figures are desired on a particular bond, "The Wall Street Journal" should be consulted. Weekly volume figures are available in "Barron's" and the Sunday issue of the "New York Times." Most libraries subscribe to these publications.

☐ No Minimum Order

Although brokerages permit clients to enter bond orders of any size, some smaller orders may be discouraged by minimum commission rates. Many brokerages have a minimum commission of $7.50 to $10.00 per bond, with minimum commissions *per transaction* of $25.00 to $30.00. Nevertheless, listed bonds can be purchased in any amount by which they are offered for sale.

Prior to placing an order for bonds, the investor should always inquire what constitutes a "transaction" for purposes of commission charges. One firm may require that all bonds trade at the *same time* in order to be considered within one transaction, while another firm may combine trades in the same bond *during the entire trading day* into one transaction.

☐ Collateral Value

There are few sources of loans which can be processed quicker and with less paperwork than those on listed securities at a brokerage. If these securities are held at one's brokerage in "street name" and a signed "customer's loan agreement" is on file, a customer can secure a loan simply by placing a telephone call or by dropping by the brokerage office to pick up a check.

The loan amount can be any figure up to the maximum percentage permitted by the Federal Reserve. The loan rate on straight bonds has normally been two-thirds of their market value, while convertible bonds have had a 50 percent loan value.

Securities held in "street name" are those which the brokerage has not had transferred into the client's name. If securities are held by the brokerage in the customer's name, they must be endorsed or a "bond power" must be signed before they can be used as collateral.

A "customer's loan agreement" is the form by which the client accepts and acknowledges the terms of security loans. This form authorizes interest charges (which can vary widely among firms) and permits the firm to sell the collateralized bonds if their value should approach or fall below the loan amount. Customers are always given the option of depositing additional funds or securitites to avoid such sales. This same form is used to establish margin accounts.

While bonds are held as collateral, the customer still retains the right to sell their bonds at any time. Interest coupon payments can be received by the customer or used to reduce the loan.

In 1979 a proposal was made to permit loans on many of the more widely-held unlisted bond issues. If approved, the advantage of being permitted to borrow on unlisted bonds still will *not* compensate for reduced marketability of o-t-c bonds.

*

HOW TO BUY LISTED BONDS

When an investor has chosen a particular listed bond for investment, it must then be determined how many bonds are for sale at a reasonable price.

☐ Obtain A "Quote & Size"
By asking an AE for a "Quote & Size," the investor can quickly determine how to enter their order. This will reveal how many bonds are immediately available at the lowest price.

For example, let us assume that an investor is interested in purchasing 15 Teledyne 10% 2006 bonds. Upon requesting a "Quote & Size," the following figures are received:

"91¼ to 92½, 8 by 20"

This means the bid and ask prices are $912.50 and $925.00 respectively; and the buyer wishes to purchase 8 bonds, while the seller is offering 20 bonds for sale.

Our investor could purchase 15 bonds immediately at $925.00. Before placing an order however, one should inquire what the bond's most recent transaction price is. This price is often referred to as the "last sale" or "latest trade." The last sale may have occurred at either end of the quote or between these two figures. When a bond trades only occasionally, the last sale may even be outside the quote prices.

In our example, the last sale might be at $920.00 The investor must then decide whether to buy the bonds immediately at $925.00, to attempt a purchase at $920.00, or to place an order at any other price which appears reasonable.

☐ Market Orders

If a buyer wishes to make a purchase at the ask price of a bond quote, they can direct their AE to place a "market order." This means that the buy order will be executed at the lowest price available *at the time* it arrives on the floor of the exchange. Prudent AEs write the "Bid & Ask" on their order tickets to signify to the exchange floor broker what the market order is based upon. This is an intelligent measure, as the "Bid & Ask" may change before a market order can reach the exchange floor.

☐ Limit Orders

If the buyer wishes to place a particular price limit on an order, then the order is called a "limit order." By entering a purchase limit order at a *higher* price than the current bid, the "Quote & Size" of the bond is changed. If a limit order to buy is placed at the same price as the current "Bid," then the new buyer takes priority after the earlier bid.

In discussions with an AE concerning whether to enter a "market" or "limit" order, the customer should realize that many brokerages encourage market orders by offering their AEs an increased net commission percentage for these orders versus limit orders. This commission difference may color the recommendations of the AE.

☐ "All-Or-None" Orders

For bonds where trading occurs infrequently, it may be difficult to purchase more than a few bonds at a time. As discussed earlier, this can cause problems in the area of minimum commissions. In order to avoid partial executions of limit orders, these orders can specify that they must be filled on an "all-or-none" basis. This means that the opposite party to the transaction has to match the order with an *equal* number of bonds or there will be no transaction.

A disadvantage of all-or-none orders is that they have *no priority* in the marketplace at their price limit. Other ordinary limit orders at the same price may be filled first. All-or-none orders are often used to take advantage of commission breakpoints, as many firms offer a reduced commission rate for orders of 10 or more bonds.

All brokerages can enter all-or-none orders, so investors should not wait for their AEs to suggest this type of order if they wish to use it.

☐ Discretionary Orders

In the case of bonds which trade frequently, sometimes it is wise to give an AE slight discretion in altering the initial price of an order. Usually this discretionary leeway should be no more than 1/8 to 1/4 of a point per bond. A specific time can also be stipulated before the AE can exercise this discretion.

Giving an AE more than the above-described discretion is not advisable as misunderstandings can too easily occur. Many wider forms of discretion are considered illegal by the exchanges and regulatory agencies.

*

Chapter 10

Exchange Offers

Infrequent announcements of bond-for-stock exchange offers in "The Wall Street Journal" provide *aggressive* investors unique opportunities for both capital gains and high yields. The rewards can develop quickly, however there are risks involved.

*

WHAT IS AN EXCHANGE OFFER?

The type of exchange offer to be discussed in this book is a bond for common stock transaction. There are several other types of exchanges involving bonds, however results of the bond-for-stock exchanges are more consistent and usually provide larger capital gains.

☐ Why Do Corporations Make Exchange Offers?

This type of exchange offer is made by corporations which wish to *reduce* the number of their outstanding common shares. This reduction has the effect of increasing "earnings per share" due to a lesser number of common shares to be divided into corporate net income. These corporations hope and anticipate that a higher earnings per share figure will result in an increased value for their common stock. In many cases, corporations making such offers are closely held by families of the founding stockholders.

☐ The Corporate Announcement

When a corporation wishes to announce an exchange offer, they generally issue a press release in addition to mailing notices to current stockholders and all brokerages holding "street name" stock. The usual way that interested investors can learn of these offers is by reading the "Wall Street Journal" on a daily basis.

☐ Terms Of The Exchange Offer

The offer is normally described in terms of a fractional amount of bond per one share of stock. For example, a corporation may offer *$50 face value* of a $1000 par value bond in exchange for each share of a $40 priced stock. This is *one-twentieth* of a bond ($1000 par value divided by the $50 face value) for each share of common stock; therefore twenty shares of stock would be required in order to obtain one bond in exchange.

In another example, *$10 face value* of a bond might be offered for each share of a $7 priced stock. This means that *one-hundreth* of a $1000 par value bond would be exchanged for one share of stock. In this case, one hundred shares of stock would have to be tendered to obtain one bond.

Exchange offers always specify the total number of shares which the corporation would like to receive in exchange from shareholders. If more than this preferred amount is tendered, the corporation may or may not accept the additional shares.

When corporations *do not* accept additional shares, they normally prorate all shares which have been tendered. For example, if 800,000 shares are the maximum acceptable shares and 1,000,000 shares have been tendered, the corporation will accept only 80 percent from each tendering stockholder. The 20 percent balance would be returned to shareholders within 2 to 3 weeks after expiration of the offer.

A *minimum number* of shares is normally specified also in order for the exchange offer to be effective.

A *time limit* is always set for the tendering of shares, however this period may be extended when less than the desired number of shares is received during the initial offering period. Such extensions are usually for 2 weeks to a month and additional shares may be accepted on a "first-come, first-served" basis.

☐ Inducement To Exchange Stock

The terms of most exchange offers provide a reasonable capital gain and an attractive yield to shareholders willing to tender their shares.

In the previous example where $50 face value of a bond is offered for each share of a $40 priced stock, the cost basis for one bond would be $800 ($40 times 20 shares). If research reveals that this particular bond should sell for approximately $1000 when listed, then a capital gain of $200 per bond can be projected.

In addition to this capital gain, individuals tendering stock with a $40 cost would also receive a bond which provides a superior yield in most cases. If the bond in this example was assigned a 10% coupon, then the current yield to investors with a cost basis of $800 per bond would be 12.5% ($100 coupon rate divided by $800).

Although the above example is simplified for explanation purposes, it is typical of the potential results from many exchange offers.

☐ Effect On Common Stock Price

An exchange offer announcement usually causes an immediate increase in the price of the affected stock, reflecting the benefits offered by the exchange. The amount of this price increase is influenced by several factors:

1. the possibility that too few shares may be tendered, causing the entire offer to be cancelled,
2. the possibility that too many shares may be tendered, requiring a proration of all tendered shares. Shares which are returned may have to be sold below their cost,
3. uncertainty as to where the new bond will be valued when it is eventually listed, and
4. the possibility of changes in general interest rates which may affect all bond prices.

At the conclusion of exchange offers, the price of the common stock may return to its pre-offer level; however, just as often it can appreciate to even higher price levels due to a significantly lesser number of outstanding shares. There is no dependable pattern for price action of stocks after the conclusion of exchange offers, however higher prices seem to occur more often when the corporation has an excellent record of profits and the number of tendered shares exceeds 20 percent of the previously-outstanding common shares.

*

BUYING TECHNIQUE FOR EXCHANGE OFFERS

Investors who wish to risk their capital for the potential benefits of exchange offers must be willing to do considerable research work.

☐ Reading "The Wall Street Journal"
It usually is not possible to take proper advantage of an exchange offer unless you are aware of it immediately upon its announcement. This requires a daily reading of "The Wall Street Journal." Exchange offers normally are described in very brief articles which may appear anywhere in this publication.

Necessary details may or may not be fully described in these articles. When they are not, the investor or their AE should telephone the corporation making the offer to obtain adequate data.

☐ Will The Bond Be Listed?
Occasionally, the corporation will have the same bond or a similar bond listed on an exchange already. This greatly simplifies one's research.

When the bond or a similar issue of the same corporation is not already listed, the investor must determine if the corporation intends to apply for its listing at the conclusion of the exchange offer. If listing is not planned, then the exchange offer should be avoided.

☐ Measure The Eventual Value Of The Bond
In approximately half of all exchange offers, the same bond or a similar issue is already listed which makes the determination of the bond's eventual value a simple matter.

In other cases, considerable research must be conducted

to decide where the new bond will be valued. An AE who is an expert in bonds can be invaluable in this determination. During this research, the investor must also decide if the corporation is of sufficient quality to warrant a bond investment in the first place. The largest capital gains and highest available yields usually occur in exchange offers which are made by small, relatively unknown corporations. Frequently, these corporations carry excessive risk for many bond and common stock holders, both of which the exchange offer participant may become.

□ Compute Acquisition Costs

Commissions on common stock purchases can be almost prohibitive in exchange offers unless relatively large amounts of stock are purchased. Generally speaking, enough stock should be purchased to exchange for 10 or more bonds. This may involve initial investments of at least $8000 to $9000. These amounts should not exceed 10 percent of one's investment capital in securities.

If an investor does not require the services of a bond expert, they may wish to use the services of a discount brokerage in order to reduce acquisition costs.

After computing the new bond's eventual value and acquisition costs, the potential capital gain should *exceed 15 percent* in order to justify a commitment. The expected current yield of the bond should be greater than comparable yields of similar-quality listed bonds. The current yield should be computed using the cost basis of the common stock as the bond's value.

□ Buy Stock Early

After its initial price increase, the common stock's price may begin moving slightly higher each trading day. If research justifies a commitment, it is important to purchase shares before increasing prices make the offer unattractive. Usually, purchases should be made within the *first week* of the offer, preferably within the first few days after its announcement.

Many investors attempt to make early purchases quickly with less than the maximum amount of capital they would commit to this type of risk. Later, when more data is available and if conditions warrant, they will double their commitment.

□ Watch The Stock's Volume

After the offer announcement, it is also important to

record the volume of the common stock's trading. These figures can provide a rough estimate of how many shares are being purchased for possible tendering.

If volume appears rather low and the price is still reasonable, *additional* investments may be justified. Low volume increases the likelihood that all tendered shares will be accepted.

When volume is exceptionally high, the possibility of excess tenders and consequent proration exists. In such cases, the investor must be prepared to sell unaccepted shares as soon as the ratio of any proration is announced (usually 2 to 3 days after the offer expires). It is possible to eliminate excess shares before physically receiving them back into one's brokerage account by "selling short."

Low or high volume should be measured against two factors:

1. the total number of shares desired by the corporation, and
2. the stock's normal volume previous to the offer. By comparing volume figures, it may be possible to anticipate corporate announcements and thereby act before other investors.

☐ Tender Shares Late

Once shares are tendered, normally they cannot be recovered. Only in cases of a proration or when less than the minimum acceptable number of shares are tendered are shares returned to investors.

It is best to tender shares relatively late during the offer period. The reason for this is the possibility that speculators in the common stock may drive its price *above* the equivalent exchange value of the bond. In this instance, an investor will realize more by selling their stock than by exchanging it for bonds.

When an exchange offer is on a "first-come, first-served" basis, the above advice does not apply.

*

Caution is suggested for investors using this bond investment medium. Not all exchange offers will prove profitable.

*

Chapter 11

Buying Mutual Funds & Money Funds

A discussion of bond mutual funds should include a clear understanding of the prime purpose of such funds. Most individuals may believe that mutual funds are formed for the benefit of their shareholders. This is not true. Many millions of investors can attest to the fact that they have not benefited from their mutual fund purchases. In fact, many of these investors may have lost substantial sums in mutual fund investments.

*

MUTUAL FUNDS ARE BUSINESSES

All mutual funds are formed for the prime benefit of their *managements*. Managements of bond funds may be brokerages or separate private corporations. Their purpose in forming a mutual fund is to obtain either *substantial acquisition fees* or to generate *yearly management fees.* Of course, these fees are paid by public investors.

The considerable profits derived from these fees are the main reason why mutual funds cannot match yields available in comparable quality listed and new-issue bonds. Individual investors in mutual funds assume these fees in the form of lower yields.

A few "no-load" (no acquisiton fee) bond funds do provide slightly higher yields than most other funds, but often by purchasing very low-grade bonds for their portfolios. Most bond investors would hesitate to purchase such bonds outright.

☐ Are Mutual Fund Managements Professional?

Advertising for mutual funds usually stresses the availability of professional management for investor's capital.

One of the best-known, most widely-promoted mutual funds in the mid-1960s was Manhattan Fund (a common stock growth fund). When originally issued in 1966, its acquisition price was $10.00 per share. Thirteen years later, its net asset value had declined to $3.00 per share. Results of this fund and many others have been expensive lessons for many mutual fund shareholders.

The performances of many mutual fund managements during the last 20 years have been so poor that several funds have changed *their identities* in an effort to stimulate new sales.

☐ Gimmick Funds

In order to maintain profitability during slack periods, the brokerage industry frequently creates new investment mediums for the public. Many of these unusual gimmicks have been some form of mutual fund and have included dual-purpose funds, closed-end funds, real estate investment trusts (REITs), unit bond trusts, and floating rate notes. The problems which investors have encountered with these gimmicks are discussed in Chapter 13.

*

DIVERSIFICATION — THE MAIN BENEFIT

The only undisputed benefit which buyers of mutual funds derive is diversification. By pooling investor capital, the management of a mutual fund can purchase large numbers of different bonds, thereby providing their shareholders somewhat more safety.

An investor in individual bonds might have sufficient funds to reasonably purchase only 2 to 3 different bond issues. If one of these bond issues begins to experience financial difficulties, a portion of the investor's capital might be adversely affected. When the same capital is placed in a mutual fund which owns more than 100 different bonds, the effect of a few poor investments is less serious.

However beneficial this diversification may be, it often leads to the greatest failing of large mutual funds — *a lack of liquidity*.

*

DISADVANTAGES OF MUTUAL FUNDS

There are many potential problems involved in the ownership of mutual fund shares besides the lack of liquidity. These potential problems require mutual fund owners to maintain a continuous review of general bond market conditions in order to properly preserve their capital.

☐ Lack of Liquidity

Most mutual funds have such *large* holdings that they experience difficulty changing overall investment positions quickly at reasonable prices, even when they can accurately project future interest rate levels.

If the federal government or an international event causes a sudden reversal of interest rates or strongly influences a continuing trend, most bond funds cannot take advantage of the situation (or avoid unnecessary losses in other cases).

On the other hand, an individual investor with a few different bonds will have no difficulty changing positions.

The prudent investor must maintain close watch over the general bond market in order to choose the better times in which to hold bonds, whether individually or within a bond fund.

123

☐ Poor Investments Encouraged

In an effort to maximize income, many mutual funds will place large portions of their investor capital in the higher-risk bond issues. These bond funds are often referred to as "junk bond" funds. Their sales literature suggests that diversification spreads the risk of their low-grade holdings. While this may be true, investors should carefully review the portfolios of such funds as their risk may still be excessive. As repeatedly stated, investors can obtain similar high yields in *higher-quality* bonds by managing their own bond portfolios.

When interest rates decline substantially, high-yielding bonds of acceptable quality become increasingly scarce. During these periods a mutual fund may have to increasingly turn to lower-quality issues in order to invest large sums of new investor capital. As a result the general risk of such bond funds may rise substantially. Since periods of low interest rates are often accompanied by reduced business activity, this may be the worst time to be purchasing lower-grade bond issues. It would be far better for bond investors to upgrade the quality of their holdings at these times.

☐ Bargain Bonds May Be Unavailable to Bond Funds

A close observer of daily trading activity in bonds will frequently notice sharp, temporary declines in various bond issues. In the absence of adverse corporate news, such price declines may signify nothing more than an anxious seller who desired to raise cash quickly. Within a short period of time, often only a day or two, the prices of many of these bonds will fully recover.

Mutual funds can rarely take advantage of these price declines as the number of available bonds is generally too few to make such purchases economical for a bond fund. The average bond holding at most funds may vary from 100 to 1000 bonds.

Individuals, of course, can easily take advantage of these bargains.

☐ Acquisition Fees

If the preceding factors do not discourage a potential mutual fund buyer, the commissions for purchasing many funds will. Brokerage-marketed mutual funds have acquisition fees which are often the equivalent of an *entire year's in-*

terest income from the mutual fund. Buyers of such funds sacrifice a year's worth of interest in the form of a commission immediately upon their purchase. This is not a good beginning for any income investment.

"Salesmanship" accounts for many purchases of these high-commission mutual funds, as well as investor ignorance of alternative investments.

*

BUYING BOND FUNDS

When an individual decides to seek diversification and limited management for their capital in a bond fund, their purchases should be restricted to "no-load" funds. This type of mutual fund can be acquired without an acquisition fee.

No-load funds are frequently advertised in financial magazines and business sections of major newspapers. They are not sold through brokerages.

The "Stock Guide" lists all major mutual funds, however many bond funds are not easily identified in this list. In addition, mutual funds may be listed alphabetically by their name *or* by the name of their management company. This can cause considerable confusion for potential investors who are not familiar with the mutual funds administered by various management companies. The "Stock Guide" does reveal whether acquisition fees are necessary for each fund.

The addresses for mutual funds and their managers can be obtained in the research departments at most brokerages.

☐ Obtaining The Prospectus

All mutual funds (and brokerages) are required to provide a prospectus with promotional material furnished to potential investors. This prospectus resembles other bond prospectuses insofar as clarity and ease of reading are concerned. Mutual fund promotional material usually stresses the "benefits" of such holdings in addition to providing graphs of any prior record which appears attractive.

Investors should view the sales material of several bond funds before making an investment decision. Both yield and quality of holdings should be closely scrutinized. The *smaller* a fund is, the better will be its liquidity when major portfolio changes are advisable.

Mutual fund managements which can display a successful investment record often attract large sums of additional capital from investors. This large influx of new capital may have the effect of reducing the mutual fund's ability to make timely portfolio changes in the future. Success in this instance may lessen the factor which makes success possible.

*

MONEY FUNDS

These funds are also referred to as "money market" funds due to the nature of their investments, which are usually high-quality, short-term (6 months or less) debt instruments such as U.S. Treasury bills, bank certificates of deposit, banker's acceptances, and commercial paper.

Money funds are much like mutual funds; except investor capital is not meant to fluctuate in value. Regardless of changes in interest rates, an investor should be able to withdraw the same amount of capital which was initially invested.

During periods of rising interest rates, potential bond investors should consider placing their investment capital into money funds. Until interest rates stop increasing, a money fund should maintain one's capital intact while providing yields which keep pace with increasing interest rates. Money funds were a popular place to deposit cash during the rising interest rates of the late 1970s. During 1979, deposits in money market funds quadrupled from $10.9 billion to $42 billion. By mid-March of 1980, these deposits had increased to $60 billion.

☐ Benefits Of Money Funds

Placing funds in a money fund is like having a savings account with a floating interest rate, in which there is no minimum holding period. Basically, the advantages a money fund can offer are:

1. a yield which is continually adjusted as the fund acquires new short-term debt instruments, of particular benefit during periods of increasing interest rates,
2. quick availability of an investor's capital as withdrawals can be made by written request, *instantly*

by a telephone call, or by writing of a check (interest continues to be earned until the check clears),

3. except for "weekend" deposits, there is no minimum time period for investments and consequently no penalty for withdrawing capital whenever an investor wishes,

4. no acquisition fee or redemption charge is made, although a yearly management fee is levied (usually 3/4 of 1%, or less),

5. to date, capital has been placed in very short-term securities of high quality, thereby enabling investors to withdraw the same amount of capital as has been originally deposited into money funds.

Other benefits are daily compounding of interest, availability of payroll deduction plans, and systematic withdrawal plans.

☐ Sources Of Money Funds

Many brokerages offer clients "in-house" money funds, whose minimum investments are normally much lower than those of independent money funds. By providing ready access to these funds, brokerages earn handsome management fees from their customers in addition to keeping customer capital close-at-hand for possible re-investment into stocks or bonds.

There are numerous other privately-managed money funds, as most mutual fund management firms also have a money fund available for their shareholders. Advertisements for these funds appear frequently in financial sections of major newspapers and magazines. These advertisments often include a toll-free telephone number for customer inquiries.

Before withdrawing funds from a money fund, the investor should check possible limitations on when interest is earned *prior* to withdrawals. Several funds do not pay interest on weekends when a withdrawal is made on a Monday. This is meant to discourage short-term deposits which might be made on Fridays for withdrawal on the following Monday (prior to the clearing of the depositor's check at the money fund's bank).

☐ Risks Of Money Funds

The risks of money funds depend to a large degree on the nature of their investments. There are a few circumstances which *might* expose assets of money funds to minor risk.

When interest rates enter a declining phase, some money fund managements may be tempted to reach for higher yields by purchasing *lower-quality* debt instruments. On rare occasions, corporate problems surprise even the "experts." If such problems affect the value of a money fund holding, capital losses might occur which would be shared equally by all investors.

Another potential problem during declining interest rates is the possibility that some money fund managements might purchase *longer term* debt in order to maintain higher yields. If interest rates suddenly reverse and begin increasing rapidly, some risk to investor's capital may occur. The longer term debt will decline in value as interest rates move upward. If investor's then begin making heavy withdrawals, they may reduce a fund's assets quicker than this debt is maturing. Some of the long-term debt may have to be *sold* at prices which are below its cost basis. Resulting losses would be automatically passed on to shareholders.

Robert J. Samuelson, economist for the "National Journal," points out another danger which investors might encounter in the future:

> "... as the funds expand, they will not only attract less knowledgeable investors but also induce the creation of more commercial paper and certificates of deposit. Quality may suffer."

The possibility that the above risks might cause investor losses is relatively slight. Any money fund management foolish enough to commit these mistakes would gain considerable adverse publicity, causing investors to quickly withdraw their capital.

The most probable risk to holders of money funds is the "cost" of lost opportunities in a bond market when interest rates enter a declining phase. When investors retain their capital in money funds during these periods, they receive a steadily declining interest rate. In the past, yields of money funds have declined to a level even lower than ordinary passbook rates at banks and savings and loans. When interest rates begin to decline, investors should consider the purchase of long-term bonds in order to lock-in high yields and to enjoy any capital gains which may accrue.

In March of 1980, the Federal Reserve required money funds to deposit 15 percent of all *new* deposits with the federal government. Reaction by managements of money funds varied. Many banned new deposits in order to maintain high competitive yields, and a number of these managements made plans to form new money funds for their new deposits. Of course, newly-established money funds will yield considerably less if only 85 percent of depositor's funds are permitted to earn interest.

A number of other money funds continued to accept new deposits and simply combined 85 percent of these new funds with their earlier deposits. Some larger funds have stated that they expect little dilution of their high yields, which is possible as long as their pre-March 1980 depositers withdraw little capital and post-March 1980 deposits remain relatively minor.

As money funds with less than $100 million in assests are currently exempt from this 15% reserve requirement, the smaller funds might be considered also.

Potential investors may obtain without charge a list of money market funds and their toll-free telephone numbers by writing:

> Investment Company Institute
> 1775 K Street N.W.
> Washington, D.C. 20006

Chapter 12

Buying Tax-Free Bonds

Tax-free bonds are also known as "tax-exempt" or "municipal" bonds. They are issued by cities, counties, states, and agencies created by these government bodies. Their income is always free of federal taxation and is generally free of state taxation if the residence of the investor is the same as the state in which the bond is issued.

Individual investors will find that the municipal bond market differs markedly from the corporate taxable bond market. Prices are quoted in different terms, these quotes vary widely among brokerage firms, and virtually no research is available to the public on municipal bond issues.

These differences are due to the fact that the municipal bond market *principally* serves institutions. In 1979, banks and insurance companies purchased approximately 75 percent _____ ion of new-issue municipal bonds. A fair p_____ ing bonds were bought by bond mutual fu_____

_____ tors in both high and medium income tax _____ well to learn how the tax-free bond mark _____ ubstantial tax savings are available to many _____ rs who may be hesitant to enter this investn _____ o a lack of understanding concerning its c _____

*

TYPES OF MUNICIPAL BONDS

Currently, there are more than 20,000 different issuers of municipal bonds, with more than 50,000 separate bond issues outstanding. Due to the permanence and security of most municipal bond issuers, these bonds are considered to be higher quality than comparably-rated taxable bonds issued by business corporations.

Municipal securities are categorized by the form of security backing each issue. This may be the taxing authority of a city, county, or state; or it can take the form of revenues resulting from use of facilities financed by the bonds.

☐ General Obligation Bonds

General obligation (G.O.) bonds are secured by the full taxing power and credit of their issuers. G.O. bonds normally include direct issues of different levels of government, school districts, and water districts.

Some G.O. bonds are called "limited" general obligations if their security is restricted to a particular tax such as property taxes. When the financial backing of a G.O. bond is limited, it is wise to determine how much of the taxing power of the issuer remains uncommitted. In some cases, the remaining reserve may be barely adequate for coverage of new bond issues.

☐ Revenue Bonds

These bonds are usually secured by the revenue or fees which result from use of the facilities financed by the bond issue. This term may also be used to describe any bond which is not a general obligation of a city, county, or state.

Hospitals, parking facilities, public utilities, educational facilities, redevelopment agencies, transit authorities, airports, ports, industrial facilities, and urban improvements are normally financed by the issue of revenue bonds. Not all of these categories are always revenue bonds however, as a city or county may choose to provide direct backing for such bonds thereby making them general obligations. The reason for this additional coverage is usually to obtain a lower interest rate or to make financing possible when revenues from a facility are considered questionable.

Most revenue bonds are aptly described by their titles. A few of these bonds are discussed in some detail due to their popularity with investors.

☐ Redevelopment Agency Bonds

These bonds are also called "tax allocation" bonds and are secured by a portion of the property taxes levied on redeveloped property. Due to such redevelopment, the property normally increases in value substantially resulting in higher property taxes. It is the *increase* in these property taxes which secures the bonds.

Since this type of bond is normally used to assist in the construction of commercial enterprises (frequently large shopping malls), it is important for investors to determine that the economic needs of nearby communities will justify such redevelopment. In recent years some states have passed new laws restricting the amount of yearly property tax increases, another factor which should be reviewed when this type of bond is considered.

☐ Airport Bonds

There are two types of airport bonds. One type is often issued for the construction of parking facilities and other *general usage* buildings. Another type of airport bond may be issued for facilities which will be leased to a particular *airline,* and their security is the leasing contract with the airline. As such, they depend on the financial status of a private corporation, therefore the airline leasing such facilities should have a satisfactory record of profitability. This is not always the case in the airline industry.

A serious drawback of a bond issued for facilities to be leased to an airline is the fact that its interest is *not* exempt from state taxation. Yields of these bonds must be slightly higher than similar-quality bonds to compensate the investor for this disadvantage.

☐ Industrial Revenue Bonds

Industrial revenue bonds are usually issued by local governments who wish to encourage the establishment of new industry. Factories are built with the proceeds of such bonds and then leased to the private corporations. When these corporations are of good quality, their industrial revenue bonds may also be acceptable risks. As with the airport bonds which are leased to airlines, industrial revenue bonds are not exempt from state taxation.

Due to the large variety of municipal bonds and the lack of comparative financial data, quality ratings of these bonds are very important in assessing their desirability.

*
QUALITY RATINGS

The rating system for tax-free bonds is similar to that of taxable bonds. The top three categories (AAA, AA, and A) are reserved for the most secure issues, differences in ratings often being due to the size of the issuer more than any other factor. Most general obligation bonds of medium to larger cities are rated in one of these three categories.

The next category (BBB or BAA) normally encompasses bonds issued by smaller cities and many revenue-producing facilities. Individuals should not consider tax-free bonds having a rating below this level. Ratings are listed in the "Bond Guide."

Normally, purchases of municipal bonds should be made from those which are "local" to the investor. In this way their stability and continuing safety can be easily monitored.

☐ Municipal Bond Insurance

If tax-free bond issuers are willing to pay the necessary

fees, they can have the principal and interest guaranteed for their new-issues. Many "normally" lower rated ('A' and 'BBB') bond issuers choose to purchase this insurance coverage as it assures a higher quality rating of 'AAA' or 'AA,' depending on which insurer is utilized. Of course, a higher quality rating enables the bond issuer to sell bonds at a much lower interest rate than would otherwise be possible.

In 1978, slightly more than 2 percent of the $45.9 billion of new tax-free bond issues had this coverage. Most of these issues were either general obligations or local public utilities.

The two private corporations now insuring municipal bonds are the Municipal Bond Insurance Association (MBIA) and the American Municipal Bond Assurance Corporation (AMBAC). MBIA is a pool of insurance companies composed of Aetna Casualty & Surety, Fireman's Fund Insurance, Aetna Insurance, and United States Fire Insurance. This corporation charges a premium ranging from 0.5% to 2.0% of the principal and interest of a bond issue, which results in a 'AAA' rating by Standard & Poor's Corporation.

The other insurer (AMBAC) is a subsidiary of a private company, MGIC Investment Corporation. AMBAC provides the same coverage to tax-free bond issuers, in addition to furnishing similar insurance to individuals, banks, and other owners of municipal bonds. Their premiums for G.O. and public utility bonds range from 0.4% to 1.75%, with higher premiums for non-utility revenue bonds. Standard & Poor's rating service assigns a 'AA' rating to bonds insured by AMBAC. It is interesting to note that the bonds of AMBAC's parent corporation (MGIC Investment) are rated 'A' by Standard & Poor's.

At the time this book is published, the other major rating service (Moody's) does not re-adjust their ratings for municipal bond issues carrying insurance coverage. As a result, bond issuers purchasing this insurance rarely apply for a rating by Moody's.

Note: Investors should not assume that all bond issues from the same tax-free bond issuer will have the same quality rating. New bond issues may carry this insurance while previous issues do not.

*

COMPUTING BENEFITS OF TAX-FREE BONDS

Most references state that a single person must earn over $15,000 and a married couple should earn over $30,000 before tax benefits can be derived by the purchase of tax-free bonds. This generalization applies only to investors who are knowledgeable and confident in the area of *taxable* corporate bonds.

There are many individuals who may hesitate to purchase taxable corporate bonds due to a lack of experience in investing and/or a preference for localized investments such as savings accounts, U.S. savings bonds purchased locally, second trust deeds, etc. For an investor with these preferences, the purchase of local tax-free bonds may provide a substantially higher after-tax income than other nearby alternatives. A tax-free yield of 7% to 9% in a local municipal bond is far superior to a *fully taxable* 5½% rate in a savings account. It is also superior to many longer term yields offered by savings institutions.

☐ Computing Your Own Tax Benefit

Knowing your own tax bracket, it is a simple matter to compute comparable yields for tax-free bonds *and* taxable bonds (or other taxable sources of interest). If an investor is in the 35 percent tax bracket, the *reciprocal* of this percentage should be divided into a current tax-free yield to obtain its equivalent taxable yield.

For example, let us assume that the above investor is considering a tax-free bond yielding 7% and wishes to know how this yield compares to taxable yields. The reciprocal of 35 percent is 65 percent (or 0.65). When 0.65 is divided into 7%, the result is *10.77%*. This means that a tax-free yield of 7% is equivalent to a taxable 10.77% yield. If corporate bonds of similar quality are yielding only 10%, then the municipal bond in this case is clearly the better yield on an after-tax basis.

In another example, let us assume that the investor is in a 30 percent tax bracket and acceptable tax-free bonds yield 6.5%. After dividing 6.5% by the reciprocal of 30 percent, we find that the equivalent taxable yield is *9.29%*. If taxable bonds of similar quality are offering 10% yields, then the investor would earn more interest on an after-tax basis in taxable corporate bonds.

□ General Comparison Table

The following table provides equivalent tax-free and taxable yields:

	Tax Bracket:	24%	28%	32%	37%	43%	49%
Tax-Exempt Yields	TAXABLE EQUIVALENT YIELDS						
5%	.... 6.58%	6.94	7.35	7.94	8.77	9.80
6	.... 7.89	8.33	8.82	9.52	10.53	11.76
7	.... 9.21	9.72	10.29	11.11	12.28	13.73
8	.... 10.53	11.11	11.76	12.70	14.04	15.69
9	.... 11.84	12.50	13.24	14.29	15.79	17.65
10	.... 13.16	13.89	14.71	15.87	17.54	19.61

*

PRICING IN THE MUNICIPAL BOND MARKET

All municipal bonds trade in the over-the-counter market. Normally, brokerage prices quoted to the public for the purchase or sale of tax-free bonds are independent judgements of managers or traders at regional municipal bond departments. If an investor requests quotes on a tax-free bond from 5 brokerages, it would be normal to receive 5 different quotes. These quotes might vary as much as $30 to $40, reflecting the varying willingness of each municipal bond department to own a particular bond issue and different pricing policies.

Individual AEs can also influence these quotes by adjusting the amount of commission to be charged the customer.

□ The Spread

The "spread" is the difference between the bid and ask prices of a bond and is a good measure of its marketability. Narrow spreads ($10 to $15) indicate better marketability and attractiveness than bonds having wider spreads.

The spread serves two purposes for brokerages. The commission for the purchase or sale of a bond is contained within this spread; which explains why commissions rarely appear on confirmation statements received by tax-free bond customers.

136

The spread also provides some leeway to brokerages in order to compensate for adverse price movements in the general bond market. There is financial risk to brokerages which maintain sizeable inventories of tax-free bonds for sale to their customers. Bond inventory values change constantly, requiring a municipal bond department manager to exercise careful judgement to avoid serious inventory losses. Investors should realize that some brokerages attempt to pass inventory losses on to their customers in the form of non-competitive prices. Most customers will not know whether a quoted price is competitive unless they obtain a few quotes from other sources.

The market in municipal bonds is unique within the securities industry for the degree of bargaining in which a customer can and should engage when buying and selling bonds. As each brokerage sets their own prices, the careful investor must be prepared to do some "comparison shopping" and frank bargaining when considering portfolio changes.

*

HOW TO BUY MUNICIPAL BONDS

The municipal bond investor should begin an investment program slowly, as poor value in bonds must be avoided as well as excessive commissions.

☐ Finding A Brokerage And A Bond Specialist

Initially, an investor should deal with several different firms in order to:

1. obtain a wide variety of quotes, and
2. locate a specialist in municipal bonds.

Over a period of time, it may become evident that one of the firms generally furnishes more reasonable quotes than the other firms do. Hopefully, the investor will also be able to locate an AE who is knowledgeable in municipal bonds at this firm. A professional AE will be capable of discerning good values for clients and can assist customers in avoiding various pitfalls. Chapter 14 suggests a procedure for finding acceptable AEs at reasonably good brokerages.

☐ Obtaining Quotes On Municipal Bonds

The bond buyer should ask each brokerage to furnish a brief price list (5 or less) of the highest yielding bonds within a particular:

1. maturity (5, 10, 15, 20, 25, or 30 years), and
2. quality rating (usually 'A' or 'BBB' is adequate for most individual investors).

It should require no longer than 24 hours for an AE to compile such a list for a client. It is common practice to quote municipal bond prices in terms of their "yield to maturity." The investor should specifically request the *actual dollar price per bond also* whenever quotes are provided.

☐ Offering Sheets

Some AEs simply furnish customers a copy of their municipal bond offering sheet, which will include their local inventory of bonds. It may also provide a brief list of up-coming new-issues.

Prices for the same bond issue should not vary by more than $15 per bond among different brokerages. Firms which consistently price their bonds over those at other brokerages can be readily identified by comparing offering sheets. Quite often these offering sheets are marked "Not For Customer Distribution," however most AEs will furnish them to customers, especially if they have nothing to hide. The last column on these sheets usually lists commissions paid for each bond, in coded form.

When a customer has developed good rapport with an AE, it may be possible to obtain some flexibility in the prices listed on these offering sheets.

☐ The "Blue List"

The "Blue List" is published each working day and lists all municipal bonds which brokerages and banks wish to advertise for sale. Most large brokerage offices subscribe to this publication and occasionally a recent copy can be obtained by an interested customer. The latest issue should be available for customer review at the brokerage office.

This publication quotes bonds mostly in terms of their

yield to maturity instead of dollar prices. Brokerages use "Bond Table" books to convert these quotes into dollar figures. The value of the "Blue List" is that its quotes are as near to "fair market values" as can be obtained on a broad, daily basis. For this reason, some firms may hesitate to make this list available to customers.

When an attactive bond is located in the "Blue List," the AE can be asked to purchase it for the customer. The quoted price in this publication includes a nominal commission ($5 to $10) for the AE. Any additional commission which is added to the price of a "Blue List" bond should not exceed $10.

☐ New-Issues

This is often the best source of municipal bond investments, as the price is set by the underwriting brokerage group and seldom varies among brokerages. Little or no accrued interest is involved and most offerings are priced at par which greatly simplifies the purchase for both brokerage and customer.

It is still important to have a professional AE when buying new-issues, as some new-issues may provide lower yields than similar-quality bonds found in the "Blue List." Reservations for tax-free new-issues should be made just as they are for taxable new-issues.

☐ When You Sell Your Tax-Free Bonds

Always obtain a minimum of *three quotes* when selling tax-free bonds. When asking for these quotes, do *not* reveal whether you are a buyer or a seller. This might adversely affect the quote you are furnished (the spread may be wider if your intentions are known). Upon receiving your quotes, be prepared to bargain. Quite often, the amount being bargained over is part of the commission rather than value in the bond, although few brokerages or AEs will acknowledge this.

*

TAX-FREE BOND FUNDS

Virtually all brokerages offer mutual funds containing only tax-free bonds. Often these bond funds are called "unit trusts." Municipal bond funds which have no acquisition fees are advertised frequently in major newspapers.

When an investor wishes to own tax-free bonds via a mutual fund, they should assure that the mutual fund they purchase contains bonds *issued only* in the state of which the investor is a resident. Otherwise, the investor may have to pay state taxes on interest received from the mutual fund.

Investors should also review the portfolio of any fund before investing in order to avoid extremely low-quality bonds which were difficult to profitably sell to the public by other means. This may occur in mutual funds sold through brokerages more often than it occurs in "no-load" funds. It is difficult to ascertain when this has happened, but investors can review portfolios of funds for *low-rated* revenue bonds issued for athletic stadiums, convention centers, racetracks, and similar facilities.

*

AN I.R.S. TAX-TRAP IN MUNICIPAL BONDS

Some individuals or married couples with taxable incomes well above the 30 percent tax bracket still *should not* purchase or own municipal bonds. Although the following "tax-trap" may arise only during personal income tax audits, it is best to be properly prepared for such experiences.

☐ Borrowing To Make Other Investments

If you have borrowed to make other investments, the ownership of municipal bonds may seriously affect the *tax deductibility* of the interest charged on these loans.

For tax-free bond owners, the following investments may result in the disallowing of part or all of related interest deductions:

1. loans to purchase municipal bonds,
2. loans to purchase other securities,
3. debt incurred due to participation in limited-partnership tax shelters,
4. loans in which municipal bonds are used as collateral, and
5. loans in which the investor cannot prove the borrowing wasn't made to avoid selling one's municipal bonds.

It does not matter which comes first, the loan or the purchase of the tax-free bonds. Loans for conducting a personal trade or business may also be affected by this rule unless the investor can demonstrate to the I.R.S. that the need for the loan could not have been anticipated at the time the tax-free bonds were purchased.

This rule does not apply for loans involving home ownership, vehicles, or other consumer items purchased on an installment basis. It also doesn't apply where municipal bonds are less than 2 percent of an investor's total investment portfolio.

When an investor believes they might be affected by this particular problem, they should immediately consult with a qualified tax accountant or attorney.

*

Chapter 13

Watching Out For
Wall Street's Gimmicks

Whenever volume slows on Wall Street, marketing personnel work harder at devising new investment ideas to entice investors into committing their capital. Some of these new ideas may have merit, however most seem to be designed to benefit the brokerage industry more than the investor.

A number of these investment ideas are meant to attract funds from the income-oriented investor. They have included:

1. dual-purpose funds,
2. real estate investment trusts,
3. unit investment trusts,
4. closed-end bond funds,
5. floating rate notes and bonds, and
6. financial futures.

Both the benefits and limitations of these investment mediums are frankly discussed.

*

DUAL-PURPOSE FUNDS

The major dual-purpose funds were issued in 1967, the year following the 1966 bear market. They included American DualVest, Gemini Fund, Hemisphere Fund, Income & Capital Shares, Leverage Fund, Putnam Duofund, and Scudder Duo-Vest Fund.

These funds have a fixed number of shares and are operated by a management company similar to other mutual funds. Their shares are listed on the New York Stock Exchange, with the exception of Putnam Duofund which is over-the-counter.

The distinctive feature of these funds is that they have two *different* classes of shares:

1. income shares, and
2. capital shares.

Each class of shares provided half of the initial capital. The plan was for the income shareholders to receive all of the income generated by the total capital (after management expenses) *and* the capital shares would receive all the appreciation, if any.

☐ Supposed Benefits Of Dual Funds

If the assets of a dual fund were invested in securities yielding 6%, then the *income shares* would receive a 12% yield (less expenses). If the fund appreciated by 15 percent, then the net capital gain to *capital shareholders* would be 30 percent. Essentially, the potential benefits to each class of shareholders would be double what they might be in an ordinary mutual fund. This potential received heavy promotion by salespersons during the original issue of these funds. The commissions offered to brokerage salespersons were several times the ordinary commissions charged for stock purchases.

The most important benefit of dual-purpose funds is that they are all to be redeemed before or by 1985. At this time, the income share investors can recover their capital if it is still intact. Capital shareholders, of course, may be less fortunate.

143

□ Limitations Of Dual Funds

Generally speaking, security investments exhibiting a high yield have very little capital gains potential, and vice versa. Consequently, managements of dual funds would be quite fortunate to satisfy both classes of their shareholders. In an effort to meet the needs of both classes however, it is more likely that neither class would be well-served.

More than a decade after their initial issue, only one of these seven dual funds could present a creditable record. *Table I* lists the original issue price of each fund and the "net asset value" of their capital shares as of March 31, 1979. Their market prices on this date are also listed.

TABLE I.

	Issue Price	Net Asset Value	Market Price
American DualVest.........	$15.00	$11.00	$10.25
Gemini Fund...............	12.00	28.03	22.25
Hemisphere Fund...........	12.50	0.42	1.62
Income & Capital Shares.....	10.00	8.46	6.62
Leverage Fund.............	15.00	21.33	17.00
Putnam Duofund...........	10.00	11.13	10.66
Scudder Duo-Vest..........	10.00	10.44	8.37

Although 4 of these funds had higher asset values after 12 years, only one of these performances was significant and justifies its original investment.

Table II lists the March 31, 1979 yields of the *income shares,* their original issue prices, eventual redemption prices, and the year of their redemption.

TABLE II.

	Yield	Issue Price	Redemption Price	Redemption Year
American DualVest	7.1%	$15.00	$15.00	1979
Gemini Fund......	15.6%	12.00	11.00	1984
Hemisphere Fund..	8.8%	12.50	11.44	1985
Income & Capital..	10.7%	10.00	10.00	1982
Leverage Fund....	10.0%	15.00	13.725	1982
Putnam Duofund .	9.8%	19.75	19.75	1983
Scudder Duo-Vest.	9.2%	10.00	9.15	1982

The average yield of these funds after their first 12 years was 8.25%, far below what investors might have realized in bond income investments. It should also be noted that 4 of the 7 funds offer investors a redemption price which is *lower* than the original cost price of these shares.

Another disadvantage is that investors in either class of shares cannot sell their shares at their "net asset value." *Table I* shows that the capital shares of all but one of these funds sell at discounts below their actual values. Other types of mutual funds which are not "closed-end" are always redeemable at their "net asset values."

A few speculators may be interested in purchasing *capital* shares of those funds which have market prices substantially below their "net asset values." As long as stock market declines do not erase these discounts, the speculator might realize capital gains.

Investors considering dual-purpose shares should give close scrutiny to their past performance records before making any commitments. S&P sheets are available on all of them.

*

REAL ESTATE INVESTMENT TRUSTS

For investors, the advent of real estate investment trusts (REITs) in the early 1970s proved to be a *disaster*. By the end of the 1970s, the average price of REITs sold to unfortunate investors had declined *75 percent*.

The sale of REIT shares to the public at high commission rates was very popular in the early 1970s. To obtain lucrative *management fees,* large banks, insurance companies, and even brokerages rushed to sponsor various forms of REITs.

□ Supposed Benefits Of REITs

REITs were formed to give the average investor with small amounts of capital an "opportunity" to invest in real estate for either income and/or capital gains. Two basic types of REITS were sponsored:

1. equity trusts, and
2. mortgage trusts.

The *equity trusts* were to invest their capital in property and shareholders were supposed to receive a cash return due to rental income and depreciation charges. As the properties appreciated in value (hopefully), it was expected that the REIT shares would also appreciate.

In the case of *mortgage trusts,* their goal was to generate interest income by loaning capital to real estate developers. Resulting interest would then be passed on to shareholders.

□ What Really Happened?

An article in the March 19, 1979 issue of "Fortune Magazine" partially describes what really happened:

> "The industry fell into a shambles in 1974 as inflation, recession, and overbuilding combined with the high cost and scarcity of money to send the real-estate market into a full-fledged depression. The so-called mortgage REITs—particularly the short-term construction lenders—suffered the most. Leveraged to the hilt, they paid the price after the cost of their own funds soared just as their income was gouged when builders defaulted on their loans."

Most of the mortgage trusts which survived now contain large numbers of foreclosed properties and much of any income they now generate goes to financial institutions instead of their shareholders.

The REITs were permitted by their bylaws to borrow heavily from financial institutions in order to increase the amount of capital they could invest in real estate ventures. Most REITs borrowed heavily, hoping to generate more income for their shareholders (and higher management fees for themselves).

Many REITs filed for bankruptcy, including one sponsored by the third largest bank in the country, Chase Manhattan Bank. Their REIT filed for court protection under Chapter 11 of the Bankruptcy Act in February of 1979.

Perhaps, the general failure of many REITs to deliver on the promises made by brokerage salespersons was in large part due to a *surplus* of lendable funds and a scarcity of reasonable opportunities in the real estate field. When prime property locations and professional developers were committed, new REIT funds sought out poorer business risks. The

146

overall results of REITs suggest that the majority of their investments were of very poor quality.

*

UNIT INVESTMENT TRUSTS

Unit investment trusts (UITs) are fixed portfolios in which investors can purchase units of participation in denominations of $1000 each. They are unique for several reasons, one of which is that the investor is charged *two* commissions in their purchase and a *third* commission when units are redeemed.

The entire portfolio of a UIT is accumulated at its beginning, before sales to the public begin. Once sales of a particular unit begin, no further additions (or changes) are made. Therefore, no portfolio management is furnished. Instead of being managed, it is more accurate to state that UITs are simply sponsored.

Although most UITs are of the tax-free type, some are also formed with taxable bonds. Sponsors of UITs are generally large brokerages or groups of brokerages. The two largest sponsors of tax-free UITs are Merrill Lynch and John Nuveen & Company. These sponsors typically gather a portfolio of $20 to $30 million worth of different municipal bonds into a "trust," and begin offering investors units at $1000 each. Interest is normally paid at 6 month intervals.

☐ Benefits Of UITs

UITS do offer relatively high yields, although this may be at the expense of considerable quality in their holdings. The benefits of diversification are provided just as with any other "mutual fund" type of holding.

☐ Limitations Of UITs

Perhaps the most serious limitations of UITs are their forementioned acquisition charges and eventual redemption charges. When the portfolio of a UIT is formed, its selling price is arranged to include not only the offering price of individual bonds held in the UIT, but also an additional sales charge ranging from 3 to 4½ percent. We have previously learned that the *offering price* of unlisted bonds already includes a hidden commission. An additional charge of 3 to 4½ percent makes the purchase of a UIT an expensive acquisition. The total acquisition charges may represent the equivalent of a full year's worth of tax-free interest.

When units are redeemed, they are priced at the *bid prices* of the bonds held in the UIT, which may be $25 or more per unit below their offering prices. Again, a hidden commission is charged.

Compensation paid to brokerage salespersons for marketing UITs may account for the fact that by mid-1978 the public held $12.7 billion of UITS and only $2.7 billion of managed tax-free bond funds (many of which have no acquisition fees). An article in the October 2, 1978 issue of "Forbes Magazine" on the subject of UITs stated.

> "many of these funds are sold to people who do not understand what they are buying . . ."

Another limitation of UITs is the fact that they are *not managed*. If a particular type of tax-free bond or issuer experiences adverse financial pressures, the bonds remain in the portfolio. As interest rates fluctuate, the portfolio is not adjusted to take advantage of these changes either.

A serious limitation is the possibility that low-quality bonds may be placed into a UIT portfolio. The bonds placed into UITs come from 3 primary sources:

1. inventory owned by the sponsor.
2. new-issues underwritten by the sponsor, and
3. non-public offerings underwritten by the sponsor (also called "private placements").

It is normal for a UIT sponsor to place bonds within a UIT portfolio which have proven difficult to otherwise market to the public. Consequently, the portfolios of many UITs may be convenient "dumping grounds" for low-quality, hard-to-sell securities.

"Supply and demand" in the marketplace may not control the value of bonds placed in UITs. The valuation of bonds placed in UITs is *at the discretion* of their sponsors. It is unlikely that a sponsor would value their own bonds for sale to their UIT at prices which represent a loss. This possible "conflict of interest" may adversely affect public investors in UITs.

One of the worst features of UITs is how they may be discontinued. Investors can sell their units back to the UIT at anytime; however, the redemption of a UIT may also be an *involuntary action*. Sponsors have the right to end a UIT's life whenever the total principal value of a portfolio falls below a particular percentage of its original asset value. At the time this book is written, Merrill Lynch terminates its UITs when only 40 percent of the principal value remains; while John Nuveen & Company terminates their UITs at the 20 percent level. Obviously, the Nuveen UITs offer investors more protection from involuntary redemption.

After such a redemption, the UIT sponsor often places redeemed bonds into a newly-formed UIT and charges another 3 to 4½ percent commission for their sale to new investors. If a previous holder of a "redeemed" UIT wishes to re-invest their funds in another UIT, they must then pay another commission. A "repeat commission" practice similar to this was banned by the state of California several years ago; however, UITs have continued to generate repeat commissions by this method.

*

CLOSED-END BOND FUNDS

Most closed-end funds were issued following the stock market decline of 1972. Another reason for their existence are the relatively high commissions paid salespersons to market them.

Closed-end bond funds are different from most mutual funds in that they cannot be redeemed at their "net asset value." Shareholders can only sell shares in these funds to other individuals, often at substantial discounts below their real values. This protects the managements of these funds, as their shareholders cannot reduce the portfolio of an inferior-performing fund by redemptions. The previously-discussed dual-purpose funds are a specialized form of closed-end funds.

Table III lists the yields of many of the largest closed-end income funds and the discounts at which they sold below their "net asset values," as of January 18, 1980:

	Yields	Discount
American General Bond Fund ...	10.8%	-6.8%
Bunker Hill Income Sec	11.9	-15.6
CNA Income Shares	11.7	-6.7
Current Income Shares	12.2	-12.9
Drexel Bond Deb. Trading	11.5	-11.6
Excelsior Income Shares	11.8	-15.9
Ft. Dearborn Income Sec	11.1	-11.8
Hatteras Income Sec	10.7	-8.2
INA Investment Sec	11.5	-13.4
Intercapital Income Sec	11.0	-8.8
Mass. Mutual Income Inv	11.5	-16.4
Montgomery Street Income Sec ...	10.3	-7.3
Mutual of Omaha Interest Shrs ...	11.9	-11.0
Pacific American Income Shrs	11.8	-16.8
St. Paul Securities	11.1	-10.3
State Mutual Securities	11.8	-16.6
Transamerica Income Shrs	11.2	-8.0

The average yield of these funds on January 18, 1980 was
11.4%. Their average discount below their "net asset
values" was 11.7 percent.

☐ Benefits of Closed-End Funds
Their benefits are similar to those of ordinary bond
funds, primarily diversification and management of an income portfolio.

☐ Limitations Of Closed-End Funds
The management fees and operating expenses of these
funds reduce their overall yields by a considerable amount. In
January of 1979, investors could have obtained a 12½%
yield in bonds of utilities such as Alabama Power, Detroit
Edison, Consumers Power, Georgia Power, and San Diego
Gas and Electric. Many industrial bonds offered even higher
yields at that time.
The other major limitation of these funds is the discount
at which they trade below their "net asset values." Shares in
closed-end funds trade just as any other common stock on
the listed exchanges or on the o-t-c market. In addition to
their "net asset values," market supply and demand influence their selling prices. The discounts at which these

funds sell indicate how these funds are viewed in the eyes of the professionals.

Another disadvantage of these funds are the commissions charged to buy and sell their shares. Trading as common stock shares, the seller of such funds is required to pay a common stock commission rate, which is generally double or triple the rate of a normal *bond* commission. Most other types of bond mutual funds have no redemption fee; and many have no acquisition fee either.

Another indication of the unattractiveness of these funds is the fact that only one of the funds listed in *Table III* was issued after 1973 (Bunker Hill Income Securities Fund in 1974). Since then, other investment alternatives have proven superior to closed-end income funds.

'   *

FLOATING RATE NOTES & BONDS

In 1974, floating rate notes (floaters) were introduced by Wall Street brokerages. Their sponsors were large banks and insurance companies. Almost $100 million worth of these notes were issued in 1974, although virtually none were again issued until 1979.

Initially, these were short-term obligations (less than 10 years) with variable interest rates. Every 6 months, their yields would be re-computed to provide a slight premium above the current return of U.S. Treasury bills. After a minimum holding period, most of the early floaters could be redeemed at par at the same intervals that yields were adjusted.

☐ Benefits Of Floaters

During periods of high or increasing interest rates, these instruments could provide a fair yield as long as U.S. Treasury bill rates remained at high levels. *At the time* floaters were first introduced, they provided a better yield with protection of capital than most other alternatives which were available to the public.

☐ Limitations Of Floaters

There were several disadvantages to early floaters and many still persist, though the newer issues have been improved somewhat.

151

By yielding a slight premium over U.S. Treasury bill rates, their yields were rather poor over the long run. As U.S. Treasury bills are considered among the safest income investments due to their short-term nature and their issuer, they pay the *lowest* yield of any debt instruments. During the first 4 years of their existence, floaters yielded 0.82 of a percentage point less than telephone bonds.

Another problem was that floaters could be redeemed at 6 month interevals only. If investors wished to recover their capital between these intervals, they were required to pay a brokerage commission to sell their notes — sometimes at prices less than par.

During periods of declining interest rates, yields of floaters would also decrease. Capital gains which normally occur in the bond market during these periods would not be realized by investors who retained their capital in floaters.

The new floaters introduced in 1979 have minimum interest rates in order to avoid extremely low yields during periods of declining interest rates; however, their redemption features are not as advantageous as earlier floaters.

Perhaps the marketing success of the newer floaters is attributable to commissions paid salespersons for selling them. *No commissions* are received by salespersons who recommend that their clients place capital in *money funds,* which are far superior to floaters (see Chapter 11).

*

FINANCIAL FUTURES

On March 1, 1979, the directors of the New York Stock Exchange announced that they had authorized the allocation of $12.4 million to finance the establishment of an exchange for trading in "financial futures." The Chicago Board of Trade (largest commodity futures market) and the American Stock Exchange preceded the New York Stock Exchange in creating markets for financial futures.

Financial futures permit speculators to gamble on possible changes in future interest rate levels. Earlier chapters have discussed the difficulty of anticipating changes in long-term or short-term interest rates. Persons taking a position in a futures contract hope to benefit by the tremendous leverage permitted by these exchanges. The speculator need deposit only 1 to 2 percent of the value of their contract position. This type of leverage permits one to double their speculative funds within a day or two. Of course, slight fluctuations can also entirely eliminate one's capital in the same short period.

In fact, financial futures (and other commodity contracts) are one of the few creations of Wall Street in which the public speculator can actually lose more than their initial deposited capital. This often occurs when a speculator fails to eliminate a losing position quickly enough. For control purposes, futures contracts have specified daily fluctuation limits. Once this limit is reached (on the upside or downside) no further trading can take place at a price beyond this limit. If a speculator has a losing position which is experiencing "limit" trading, the losses may accumulate and nothing can be done to halt their growth until the market reverses itself.

This method of speculating is very tempting to those who wish an opportunity for a *rapid resolution* of their commitment. Numerous books are available explaining theoretically how profits can be made in futures contracts. This medium is *outright gambling* and it should be avoided by anyone wishing to preserve their capital.

When reviewing a new investment idea, the wary investor should consider the following advice which appeared in a "Forbes Magazine" article on August 1, 1977:

"beware a super high-pressure salesman offering you an investment cure-all."

PART III

Establishing Your Bond Program

Chapter 14

Finding And Cultivating Your Bond Expert

A successful, long-term bond program is greatly enhanced by the services of an account executive who is highly knowledgeable in the field of bonds. Locating such an expert may require some effort. Once this professional assistance is found, it is also important to know how best to utilize such services.

*

CHOOSE THE INDIVIDUAL, NOT THE FIRM

Bond experts can be located at almost any size firm, although they seem to be more numerous in medium to smaller-size firms. Specialists in bonds are often too independent-minded for the larger, highly-organized brokerages. Some firms actually discourage such specialization, as bonds are normally not a high commission item.

In the search for a bond expert, a number of investors may prefer the convenience of a nearby brokerage office. This may be best for those investors who wish to conduct considerable research. However, many offices do not have a single salesperson who possesses adequate experience in income-oriented securities. When local firms do not have personnel trained in bonds, investors should not hesitate to contact other more distant firms. Most AEs encourage their customers to call collect when their offices are not local. Many firms maintain toll-free numbers to encourage a wider clientele.

*

CONTACTING A FIRM

Brokerage offices generally maintain a rotating roster of AEs who are responsible for handling new customer inquiries. When a particular AE is assigned to handle such contacts, this AE is referred to as the "floor broker." This term is also used to describe traders who execute orders for brokerages on the floors of the stock exchanges.

If a potential customer requests that the receptionist refer them to a bond specialist, most likely they will be referred to whoever happens to be the current floor broker instead. Of course, few AEs will admit that they possess limited experience in bonds.

☐ Ask For The Manager First

Instead of telling the receptionist of your needs, it is much better to first ask for the office manager as you will be less likely to be simply shunted to a floor broker. The manager will know the capabilities of available AEs and may refer a new bond customer to the most-qualified AE in this field.

A potential customer should be emphatic when requesting

156

a bond specialist. The office manager should be requested to provide an AE who:

1. remains abreast of new developments in the bond market,
2. is aware of all alternatives among listed and new-issue bonds, *and* taxable and tax-free bonds, and most important
3. is oriented toward servicing a clientele more interested in income investments than common stock speculations.

Most bond specialists also provide services to owners of common stock; in fact, much of their business may be conducted in common stocks. Investors should not ask for an AE who deals *exclusively* in bonds, as there are few such AEs.

By speaking to the manager first, it may also be possible to judge the quality of service offered by a brokerage office. A helpful, courteous manager probably encourages a similar atmosphere within the brokerage office.

*

WHAT TO ASK THE "BOND EXPERT" CANDIDATE

As already stressed, asking a brokerage for a bond specialist does not necessarily assure that you will be referred to one. There are a number of relevant questions, the discussion of which can reveal an AE's knowledge of income investments.

☐ Are Bonds Or Stocks Recommended For Income Needs?

Many common stock-oriented AEs may respond to this question by recommending a stock having a relatively high dividend yield. In many cases, the yield of a common stock is high due to a substantial drop in the common stock's price rather than rapid increases in its dividend rate. Such yields frequently indicate the unattractiveness of the stock and serve as a "warning" that it should be avoided.

Even new-issue common stock offerings (in which no commission is charged the customer) are usually unsatisfactory recommendations because:

1. dividends do not have the safety of bond interest payments as interest is paid before taxes, while dividends are paid after taxes,
2. dividends on common stocks are not prorated for sellers as interest on bonds is, and
3. if and when stock is sold, a higher commission rate must be paid compared to bond commission rates.

Quite often, the AE who recommends stocks instead of bonds for income investors is considering comparative commissions first and the customer's interest second.

□ What Is On The Firm's New-Issue Bond Calendar?

A bond expert will always have the list of expected new-issues for bonds close at hand. Reasonably close estimates (with one-quarter of a percentage point) of expected new-issue yields should also be available from a bond specialist.

New-issue offering sheets are usually distributed every Monday morning in brokerage offices and cover all stock and bond issues coming to market for that week. An AE who is not knowledgeable concerning bond new-issues is most likely poorly-informed concerning bonds in general.

□ Are Bond Mutual Funds Recommended?

A professional AE may hesitate to recommend bond mutual funds sold through brokerages due to their heavy commission charges. Other AEs, who cannot be bothered to stay abreast of the bond market, often recommend bond mutual funds to income-oriented clients. These AEs should be avoided for obvious reasons.

Perhaps the new bond customer should state that they "are considering a 'no-load' bond fund" and then ask their AE what other alternatives are suggested. In all fairness, an AE should not be asked to recommend a no-load fund.

□ What Is The Interest Coverage On Local Utility Bonds?

By asking this simple question, one can test the quickness and accuracy in which an AE uses the "Bond Guide." A slow response may mean that the AE doesn't have a "Bond Guide" close at hand. All bond specialists require this reference manual several times daily and will be able to respond quickly to this question.

A few common stock-oriented AEs may not know how to answer this question at all. Of course, the customer asking this question should know the answer to this type of question beforehand. In the "Bond Guide," the first column of figures after the name of the bond issuer provides the "Charges Times Earnings" record for a period of three years. These figures represent the number of times available earnings (after income taxes but before extraordinary charges or credits) cover fixed interest charges of a corporation.

☐ Is The AE Available During Non-Trading Hours?

Many stock-oriented AEs remain at their desks only during New York Stock Exchange trading hours (10 A.M. to 4 P.M., Eastern Standard Time), as they may have very little to do at their desks before or after these hours. Research, intelligent investment planning, and bonds are usually foreign subjects to such AEs. On the other hand, AEs specializing in bonds usually work full days at their offices unless they must leave for outside appointments.

There are numerous other questions which might be asked by customers seeking a bond specialist. The above inquiries should provide an accurate test in most cases.

*

CULTIVATING YOUR BOND EXPERT

Once an AE knowledgeable in bonds is located, it is important that the investor develops a good working relationship with this individual. As in any professional field, much better service will be available when a pleasant relationship prevails.

An AE is more likely to patiently explain details and the basis for particular investments to the pleasant customer; in addition to promptly furnishing S&P sheets, prospectuses, "Bond Guides," and other research material. An appreciative AE will also keep clients better-informed concerning important news announcements and relevant tax information.

One of the most important benefits which a cordial customer may receive is *early* notice of attractive new-issues. Strong new issues are usually sold-out long before they are marketed. An AE will encourage favored customers to make early reservations for these issues. Most new-issues are sold

159

on a "first-come, first-served" basis, therefore the first investors to become aware of such issues may be the only ones who benefit.

☐ When To Contact An Account Executive

When initially contacting an AE, do so either before or after trading hours of the N.Y. Stock Exchange. The numerous questions which are necessary to ask a potential AE will require more than a few minutes time. A conversation during market hours may be interrupted repeatedly by the AE's current customers. Many of these interruptions will be to discuss or place orders, which must receive priority during trading hours.

Once an account has been established, the customer should restrict conversations with their AE to *orders only* during trading hours. When contacting an AE during trading hours, do not be concerned if the AE requires more than a minute to get to you. During busy markets, an AE may have 3 or 4 clients "on hold" at one time. Rather than leave a message, it is best to remain on hold until the AE has an opportunity to pick up your line. More incoming calls may not permit an AE to return a message quickly and occasionally a message may be "garbled."

On occasions when a customer wishes to discuss other matters such as research information, understanding brokerage statements, etc., contact with the AE should precede or follow trading hours. If this is not possible, then a message should be left with the AE's secretary concerning the subject of concern, with a request that the AE contact the client as soon as convenient.

When your AE is located out-of-town, call collect for important reasons only (usually for placing orders). Most routine communications can probably be handled satisfactorily by simple letters or postcards.

☐ Place Realistic Orders

Unless the AE suggests otherwise, most orders should be placed at price levels which are within *weekly* ranges of current fluctuations. As discussed in earlier chapters, order prices should be based on information obtained from "Quote & Sizes."

☐ Don't Ask Your AE To "Watch" A Security For You

Many clients will ask their AE to "watch" a particular security to see if it becomes either underpriced or overpriced. This is very difficult for any AE who has a sizeable clientele. There are hundreds of securities which an AE's clientele may own. When a client makes such a request, the AE often assumes that the client is undecided concerning the security involved and therefore the request is simply ignored. If the client really wishes to act on lower or higher prices, then *limit* orders should be placed reflecting these intentions.

☐ Don't Require "Handholding" From Your AE

A number of clients require considerable "handholding" with their investments. They wish to be regularly reassured that they've done the right thing, regardless of who recommended the investment or how small it may be. An AE burdened with several of this type of client finds a great deal of tedious repetition in customer conversations.

Customers who continually question investments unnecessarily may find that their AEs no longer make the initial contact in communications. Of course, the time for a client to strongly question an investment is *before* it is made.

☐ Can Short-Term Fluctuations Be Explained?

It is dissatisfying to make a purchase and see the security immediately fall in value, even if temporarily. Similar disappointment may occur when a security is sold and the price increases soon thereafter. It is perfectly normal for prices to fluctuate contrary to one's best predictions on a short-term basis, and such fluctuations should not discourage one from investing in sound securities.

The experienced investor knows that on a short-term basis, prices will fluctuate the opposite of one's intentions at least *half of the time.* Actually, day-to-day decisions of other investors, who often buy or sell securities for reasons other than intrinsic value, account for the unpredictability of most short-term fluctuations.

The customer who frequently insists that their AE provide an "original" explanation for contrary price movements is asking for explanations which may not be valid or relevant. In answering such questions, AEs usually state that the "rest of the market dropped" or that some particular unforeseen news accounted for the price change. These explanations may be given simply to placate the customer until more favorable price fluctuations occur.

AEs are seldom asked to explain why a security promptly moves in its intended direction since this is considered "normal." On a short-term basis, it is normal only half the time.

As long as a client's capital is invested on a long-term basis, it should be viewed in a similar manner. As stressed earlier, the greatest concern for an investment should occur prior to the commitment of capital.

☐ Don't Expect To Bargain Over Bond Commissions

When a professional AE devotes considerable time to planning a client's investment program, it is not reasonable to request discounted bond commissions.

An active trader in sizeable bond orders (10 or more) might request some form of reduced commissions, providing orders are placed on an "All-Or-None" basis and the customer does most of their own research. Depending on the nature of one's investments, discounted commissions should be discussed when an account is first opened.

☐ Keep Track Of Your Financial Records

It is normal for customers to occasionally misplace a confirmation slip or monthly statement, and on such occasions an AE will be happy to provide additional copies. However, some customers maintain poor personal records and routinely request copies of their brokerage records at tax-time. This can be a great source of irritation to the AE *and* the AE's secretary.

☐ Refer Friends To Your Bond Expert

If a bond professional is located whose advice has proven consistently valuable, the investor should actively refer other acquaintances to this AE. This will endear a client to an AE better than any other method. Quite often, an AE considers a client who refers other clients as more valuable than other larger clients and will devote special attention to such a client.

*

Chapter 15

Establishing A Tax-Free Retirement Account

The information provided in this chapter is relatively brief and subject to change. Those wishing to benefit by retirement accounts should always verify current government regulations with their tax advisor or by contacting the Internal Revenue Service.

Brokerages, banks, insurance companies, savings and loans, and other financial institutions sponsor retirement plans and distribute relevant literature which can also be a source of up-to-date information.

*

BENEFITS OF RETIREMENT PLANS

There are several important benefits for individuals who establish retirement plans besides the accumulation of a sizeable sum for security at one's retirement.

☐ Tax Deductions

The ability to reduce one's yearly taxes is an immediate benefit. Contributions are tax-deductible and can range from 10 percent of one's income (which may be a few hundred dollars) to as much as $15,000 for self-employed persons in higher tax brackets.

Yearly tax deductions are meant to encourage individuals to establish retirement accounts. The intelligent investor will plan financial expenditures so annual contributions can be made to a retirement plan instead of paying higher taxes to the I.R.S.

☐ Tax-Deferred Income and Capital Gains

Even when tax deductions are not needed, the ability to place capital in a "tax-free" investment can be quite valuable. Taxes on income and capital gains derived from retirement accounts are *postponed* until retirement age (anywhere form 59½ to 70½ at the investor's option). This means that yearly income and capital gains accumulate on a tax-free basis each year and can be totally re-invested to generate additional capital.

If a qualifying individual has several thousand dollars in a savings account, it may be possible to *double or triple* one's after-tax income by transferring these funds to a retirement account.

☐ Additional Voluntary Contributions

Current tax law permits self-employed individuals to make "voluntary," non-deductible contributions to Keogh retirement accounts. The only condition is that the self-employed person has one other non-owner employee as a member of the retirement plan. This voluntary contribution is limited to 10 percent of earned income, not to exceed $2500. Although such contributions are not deductible, they still earn tax-deferred income and capital gains.

Unfortunately, voluntary contributions are not available to individuals contributing to IRA accounts.

☐ Estate Tax Exclusion Of Contributions

A benefit which is not widely known is the fact that funds placed in a retirement account are *not* included in one's gross estate for Federal estate tax purposes.

There are two requirements to qualify for this exclusion:

1. the beneficiary must not be the contributor's estate, and
2. benefits must be payable to the beneficiary over a period of at least 3 taxable years.

These conditions can be stipulated at the time any retirement account is established. The beneficiary can also be a trust, which may be particularly convenient for potentially large estates. In the case of Keogh accounts, a trust beneficiary can be utilized to exclude retirement proceeds from the taxable estate of the participant's surviving *spouse* also.

☐ Forced Savings Account

Many individuals have monthly contributions automatically deducted from their checking accounts, which helps solve the problem of accumulating capital for persons who find saving money difficult. By placing excess funds in a retirement account, it is also easier to resist the temptation to deplete one's savings. Savings in a retirement account may seem to be more remote and therefore less subject to withdrawal for "impulse" expenditures.

*

QUALIFICATIONS & RULES FOR AN IRA ACCOUNT

When an employee works for a firm which has no retirement plan, they should consider establishing an Individual Retirement Arrangement (IRA) account. A person can contribute to their own IRA account if they are not an active participant (for any part of the year) in:

1. a qualified pension, profit-sharing, or stock bonus plan of an employer,
2. a qualified annuity plan of an employer,
3. a qualified bond purchase plan of an employer,
4. a retirement plan established by the Federal government, a State, or a political subdivision of either,

5. an annuity contract purchased by certain tax-exempt organizations or public schools, or
6. a qualified plan for self-employed individuals (HR-10 or Keogh plan).

Yearly contributions can be made until the contributor reaches the age of 70½. These contributions must be in the form of cash (currency or checks). In 1978, legislation changed the due date for contributions to the filing date for tax returns (plus any extensions). This means the individuals who add to their retirement accounts by April 15th can take a tax deduction from their previous year's income.

☐ Company Retirement Plans With Deferred Vesting

If an employer's retirement plan requires employees to be employed for 5 to 10 years before benefits vest (before employees can be sure of receiving any part of their benefits), such employees may *not* make payments to an IRA account. Employees at these firms are considered active participants in the retirement plan as soon as they enter the plan, regardless of when they become vested.

☐ Contribution Limits

Individuals who meet the requirements for contributions can invest and deduct up to 15 percent of their compensation or $1500 per year, whichever is the lesser amount. If the employee is married and the spouse is also employed, they can each start an IRA. Combined deductions may be as much as $3000 per year.

If the employee is married and the spouse has *no* compensation, each can still start an IRA. The employee must contribute the same amount to each IRA account. In this instance, the employee can contribute and deduct up to 15 percent of the employee's compensation or $1750 ($875 to each IRA), whichever is the lesser amount.

☐ Financial Institutions Sponsoring IRAs

An IRA must be established at a financial institution where the assets are held in "trust." An individual can choose to completely control the investment of their funds or the financial institution can be given this responsibility.

Institutions sponsoring IRA plans include banks,

federally-insured credit unions, savings and loans, insurance companies, brokerages, trust companies, and trade or professional associations. The Federal government also "sponsors" an IRA alternative by offering U.S. Individual Retirement Bonds, however their yield is currently 6½% which is far too low to encourage commitments.

☐ When An IRA Must Be Distributed

While IRA funds can be withdrawn as early as the age of 59½, withdrawal of IRA funds *must* begin before the end of the year in which the participant is 70½. The distribution may be the entire interest or it may be made in periodic distributions.

If the participant chooses to receive periodic distributions, a plan must be made to distribute the entire interest over any of the following periods:

1. the participant's life,
2. the lives of the participant and spouse,
3. a fixed period not extending beyond the participant's life expectancy, or
4. a fixed period not extending beyond the joint life expectancy of the participant and spouse.

When the participant becomes deceased prior to distribution of the entire interest, the remaining interest can be applied to the purchase of an immediate annuity for beneficiaries *or* it must be distributed to beneficiaries within 5 years. If the participant is survived by a spouse and the spouse dies before the entire interest is distributed under a joint or survivor option, then the same provisions apply to the spouse's beneficiaries.

If distributions are arranged for a fixed period, as permitted in (3) and (4) above, and began before the participant's death; no annuity contract is required and installment payments over the remaining fixed period may extend beyond 5 years.

☐ Penalties For Premature Withdrawals

Premature withdrawals cannot be made *without* penalty unless the participant is disabled. Otherwise, premature withdrawals from an IRA become taxable ordinary income in the year they are taken. This is not a serious penalty, as an income tax would have had to be paid on the original contribution amount if it had not been placed into an IRA account in the first place.

To further discourage premature withdrawals, the IRS imposes a 10 percent penalty on the amount withdrawn. This also should not be considered serious, especially if the funds have been accumulating tax-free for several years. However, when funds have been in a retirement plan for only 1 or 2 years, a 10 percent penalty may negate all or most of the prior tax benefits.

For more details and updated information concerning IRA accounts, readers are advised to obtain their local toll-free IRS number and request the latest edition of IRS publication NO. 590 — "Tax Information On Individual Retirement Arrangements."

*

QUALIFICATIONS & RULES FOR SELF-EMPLOYED RETIREMENT ACCOUNTS

Self-employed retirement accounts are often referred to as "Keogh" or "HR-10" accounts. Keogh was the name of the member of Congress who sponsored the bill creating this form of account.

Self-employed individuals have a considerable advantage when establishing retirement accounts compared to persons who can only qualify for an IRA account. The maximum contribution to an IRA retirement program is $1750 (employee with non-working spouse), whereas the maximum deductible contribution for a Keogh account ranges from $7500 to $15,000.

Keogh accounts are used by self-employed professionals (lawyers, physicians, accountants, and other small businessmen.) Persons employed by owners of small businesses must receive contributions also, if they have more than 3 years service. A "year of service" means a 12-month period during which the employee has not less than 1000 hours of employment. The percentage contribution for an employee must compare to that of the self-employed owner.

There are two types of Keogh accounts, depending on the level of a self-employed individual's income. Self-employed persons earning *less than* $60,000 usually utilize a defined *con-*

168

tribution plan, and those earning in excess of $60,000 often find a defined *benefit* plan as the most suitable.

☐ **Contribution Limits Of A Defined Contribution Plan**

Most Keogh accounts are defined *contribution* plans, meaning that contributions are based solely on the amount of earned income of the self-employed person. The maximum contribution for this type of plan is 15 percent of earned income, up to a maximum of $7500.

As mentioned earlier, self-employed persons *with* an employee or employees may contribute an additional 10 percent of earned income to their retirement plans, up to a maximum of $2500. These are called "voluntary" contributions. They are *not* tax-deductible; however, their income and capital gains are tax-deferred.

A unique feature of Keogh accounts is their minimum contribution rule. If total earned income does not exceed $750, a minimum contribution can be made which amounts to 100 percent of earned income. For example, if the business generates only $500 of earned income in a particular year, the entire $500 can be placed into a retirement plan.

☐ **Penalties For Premature Withdrawals**

In addition to the IRA penalties (withdrawals become taxable ordinary income in year taken, plus a 10 percent penalty), self-employed owners withdrawing funds from their Keogh accounts are disqualified from making new contributions for a period of *5 years*. This 5-year wait does not apply to employees of the self-employed owner.

The premature withdrawal of one self-employed owner (such as in a partnership) does not affect contributions of another partner.

☐ **Defined Benefit Plans**

Persons in higher income tax brackets (over $60,000 in most cases) may wish to consider a defined *benefit* retirement plan. In this plan, an actuary determines how much of a *lumpsum* will be necessary to provide a desired monthly retirement income. After this lumpsum has been computed, the actuary then figures back from this amount to find the necessary annual contributions to eventually accumulate this lumpsum. Annual contributions will vary widely from person to person, depending upon the age of the contributor *and* their income at the time the plan begins.

Some participants in defined benefit plans are able to contribute as much as $15,000 a year into this type of plan. In some cases, the contribution may approach 100 percent of one's salary. This type of plan is especially useful to professional athletes and entertainers who often experience shorter "careers" than other working individuals.

The actuary who assists the contributor must be licensed to practice before the IRS, and all details of such plans must be approved before contributions are made. Incorporation is often advised for the owners of these plans.

There are a number of other minor differences between IRA and Keogh retirement accounts. They can be reviewed by ordering IRS Publication No. 560 — "Tax Information On Self-Employed Retirement Plans." As in the case of the IRA plans, frequent changes in IRS rules may affect self-employed retirement plans.

*

ESTABLISHING A RETIREMENT PLAN ACCOUNT

Retirement accounts can be established at numerous financial institutions.

It is recommended that retirement accounts be established at a trust company which permits the plan's securities to be held by a brokerage. There are several reasons why this should be done:

1. the contributor can then fully control investments of the retirement plan in order to maximize its growth,
1. assets at a brokerage are insured, whereas assets at a trust company may not be, and
3. a brokerage furnishes monthly statements whenever transactions occur or income accrues in an account, whereas trust companies usually furnish less frequent statements.

Most professional AEs can assist clients in establishing this type of account. Often, the necessary forms can be completed in 2 to 3 minutes.

Some brokerages may prefer that retirement account securities be held by outside trust companies. In such cases, the investor should locate a more cooperative brokerage.

☐ Transferring Retirement Accounts

Retirement accounts can be freely transferred between financial institutions, as long as the participant does not permit the assets to be placed in the participant's name *and* does not in any manner take possession of the securities.

Instructions for such transfers are similar to routine instruction for transferring securities between brokerages.

☐ No Collateral Value

If retirement accounts are pledged as collateral, it is considered a premature withdrawal by the IRS and penalties are assessable. Investors are advised to find other sources of collateral whenever possible.

Chapter 16

How To Safeguard Your Bonds

    Taxable bonds can be owned or registered in 3 basic ways. Which is most suitable will depend on each individual's goals and needs. These forms of ownership are registration:

1. in the investor's name and held by the investor,
2. in the investor's name and held by a brokerage, or
3. in the name of a brokerage — "street name."

    For *tax-free* bonds, there is usually only one form of ownership and that is bearer form (in no name). Tax-free bonds are rarely registered, as this reduces their marketability and thus their value. Municipal bond issuers also prefer that their bonds remain in bearer form, as this eliminates the need for re-registration whenever their bonds change hands.

*

WHY REGISTER BONDS IN YOUR NAME?

    The most common form of ownership is to have bond certificates registered in the name of the investor. This is routinely done following most purchases at no charge. Aside from personal preferences of each investor, there are several important reasons for registering bonds in the owner's name.

☐ Receiving Timely Interest Payments

Semi-annual interest checks are sent directly to registered owners. On the other hand, when a client's bonds are held by a brokerage in "street name," the interest checks are sent first to the brokerage. Most brokerages mail interest and dividend checks to clients on a *weekly basis,* instead of on the day they are received from the bond issuer. This can result in a 3 to 10 day delay for customers in receiving income from their investments.

☐ More Flexible Collateral

When bonds are registered in the investor's name, they can be quickly used as collateral for loans at banks and other non-brokerage institutions.

When bonds are not registered in the client's name, a brokerage may require *3 to 6 weeks* to have them so registered. This length of delay may be inconvenient to the investor.

Registered bonds can be immediately deposited in the customer's account at a brokerage in order to obtain a loan also.

☐ Maintaining Accurate Records

When several different bonds are owned, it may assist record-keeping to have all certificates registered in the investor's name.

If a customer's bonds are held in "street name" instead, several problems can occur. When interest payment dates on different bonds in the same customer account are similar or relatively close, brokerages normally combine these interest coupons for payment purposes. This can lead to investor confusion later when taxes must be computed.

Another problem occurs when clients rely on year-end brokerage statements of total yearly interest and dividends paid in a customer account. Investors should realize that these year-end statements are usually inaccurate when bond transactions have occurred. These statements never take into account *accrued interest* which is paid or received by the investor in the purchase or sale of bonds. Therefore, bond buyers may *overstate* their net interest income if they rely on these figures.

By holding all bonds in registered form, an investor can

easily keep track of all interest received as it is sent by the bond issuer directly to the investor.

Another advantage of holding your own certificates is greater privacy. Sometimes it is best not to tell commission-oriented salespersons what your holdings are.

*

KEEPING REGISTERED BONDS AT YOUR BROKERAGE

Many brokerages will hold securities which are registered in a customer's name. These certificates are usually held at the main office of the brokerage, which is normally New York City for national firms.

This is a convenient form of ownership, as the brokerage is responsible for safeguarding the certificates, while interest checks are still sent by the bond issuer directly to the investor.

When and if the customer chooses to sell such securities, it is necessary to sign a "bond power" form. This form acts as a substitute for the endorsement of the actual certificate, a necessary procedure in selling bonds registered in a customer's name. The brokerage cannot deliver a sold certificate to the buyer's brokerage until it has been properly endorsed or a matching bond power has been signed. Until such delivery can be made, the selling brokerage will not pay the proceeds of the sale to the seller.

When an owner wishes to borrow on registered bonds held at a brokerage, it is necessary to sign a bond power form for the certificates in addition to executing loan agreement forms. If the customer wishes to use their registered certificates as collateral at another financial institution, the certificates can usually be obtained by the owner within a week to 10 days.

Several large brokerages will not hold certificates which are registered in a customer's name, and some which do may levy a small service charge. If a bondholder prefers this form of ownership, they should ascertain a brokerage's policy prior to opening an account.

*

LEAVING BONDS IN "STREET NAME"
Many customers prefer to leave their certificates at their

brokerage, registered in the brokerage's name.

The main advantage of this form of ownership is that no paperwork is required when such certificates are sold. Active accounts often use this form of registration.

Another advantage is the speed in which loans on "street name" certificates can be obtained. When loan agreement forms have been previously signed, a loan can be requested by a simple telephone call.

Disadvantages of this form of ownership are the forementioned delay in receiving interest checks and potential confusion in deciphering monthly and yearly statements from brokerages.

*

INSURANCE FOR BROKERAGE ACCOUNTS

In 1970, Congress passed legislation creating the Securities Investor Protection Corporation (SIPC). SIPC is a self-regulating, non-profit corporation consisting of members of the securities industry. Although it is not a government agency, the Securities and Exchange Commission monitors some of its operations.

When a brokerage firm is in *or* approaching serious financial difficulty, the SIPC may decide the customer accounts require its protection. If such a decision is made, the SIPC applies to a Federal district court for appointment as trustee to handle to liquidation of the troubled brokerage.

Upon appointment as trustee, the SIPC may arrange for some or all of the customer accounts to be transferred to another firm which is not having financial difficulties. Customers who are involved may decide to deal with the new firm or they may transfer their account again to another firm of their own choosing.

If a customer's account is not transferred, the SIPC will send all securities registered in the customer's name (or in the process of such registration) directly to the customer. If a customer's securities are held in "street name," such certificates may also be sent to the customer by the SIPC, providing they are *fully available*. If they are not fully available, remaining security claims are insured up to a maximum of $100,000. Claims for cash are insured up to $40,000.

*

REPLACING A LOST CERTIFICATE

As a matter of course, the majority of bond owners will adequately safeguard their certificates in a safety deposit box. Perhaps an explanation of how lost certificates must be replaced will encourage *all* bondholders to properly safeguard their certificates.

When repeated searches do not turn up a lost certificate, the registered owner should notify their AE. The AE can assist the customer in filing of the necessary forms for replacement of the certificate. In most cases, it is necessary for the customer to pay a fee of approximately 3 percent of the bond's value as a "surety bond." On a bond certificate valued at $10,000, this surety fee would amount to $300.

It is important for the customer to ascertain that the brokerage did, in fact, mail the certificate to the customer. When such a certificate appears to not have been delivered by the U.S. Post Office, then the brokerage will normally replace the certificate *at no cost* to the customer.

Many firms request customers to sign receipts for certificates upon their delivery in order to prove that they have been received by the customer.

It usually requires several months to replace a lost certificate, as the board of directors of most corporations must approve such replacements. During this period, the customer cannot sell their securities; however, they will continue receiving scheduled interest payments (unless the certificate is a tax-free bond with attached coupons).

A recurring theme of this book has been the necessity for thoroughly investigating all investment options prior to committing one's capital. Information provided in this book should enable investors to make intelligent choices of these options.

Hopefully, readers will also be able to distinquish between the many reasonable and unreasonable bond investment ideas which will surely be introduced in the future.

A philosopher of ancient times once dared the paradox that the greatest good fortune lies, not in having the most possessions, but in having the fewest wants.

(Definitions provided are as the terms apply
within the general subject matter
of the book)

Glossary

ACCRUED INTEREST—accumulated interest since a bond's previous interest payment date.

ASK PRICE—the selling price of a bond, the lowest selling price on a bond exchange.

BASIS POINTS—the change or difference between two percentage yields.

BEARER BOND—a certificate which has no owner name on its face.

BID PRICE—the buying price of a bond, the highest buying price on a bond exchange.

BOND POWER—a form, the signing of which is the equivalent of endorsing the back of a certificate.

CALL PROTECTION—the period of years after initial issue of a bond before it can be redeemed.

CONFIRMATION SLIPS—transaction notices mailed to buyers and sellers of securities.

COUPON—the dollar amount of yearly interest paid by a bond, also a bond's percentage yield at par.

CURRENT YIELD—obtained by dividing a bond's coupon by its current price.

DISCOUNT BOND—bond selling below par ($1000).

EARNINGS PER SHARE—profits of a corporation, obtained by dividing net income by the number of outstanding common shares.

EXECUTION DATE—date of a security transaction at the marketplace.

FEDERAL FUNDS RATE—interest rate paid by banks for short-term borrowings (usually overnight).

FULL-SERVICE FIRMS—brokerage firms offering complete customer services in all security fields.

INTEREST CHARGES Versus EARNINGS—the number of times that earnings cover fixed interest charges of a corporation.

INTEREST COVERAGE—see above.

INVESTMENT VALUE—the value of a convertible bond when or if it sells solely on the basis of its yield, usually when its common stock is selling substantially below the bond's conversion price.

LIMIT ORDER—a purchase or sell order placed at a particular price.

MARGIN ACCOUNT—an account at a brokerage in which a client can purchase securities without paying in full (interest is charged on the unpaid balance).

MARKET ORDER—a purchase or sell order placed to trade immediately at the best price available.

"OPEN MARKET" PURCHASES—security purchases by a corporation in the marketplace for the purpose of redeeming bonds.

OVER-THE-COUNTER—the unlisted market for securities.

PARTIAL EXECUTION—an execution when less than the total volume of an order is executed.

PAR VALUE—the value of $1000, at which most bonds are initially issued.

POINT—a "ten dollar" unit value of a bond.

PRIME RATE—generally the loan rate offered by a bank to its strongest financial customers.

PRORATION—upon the sale of a bond, the proportionate dividing of interest between its seller and buyer.

REFUNDING—the re-financing of a bond issue in order to take advantage of lower interest rate levels.

REGISTERED BOND—a bond registered in the name of the owner or the owner's agent (a brokerage or other financial institution).

SEASONED BONDS—bonds which are no longer new-issues.

SELLING SHORT—a transaction in which the sale of a security precedes its purchase.

SETTLEMENT DATE—the date by which the buyer must pay for a purchase and the seller must deliver the sold security, usually 5 business days following the security's execution date.

SPREAD—the difference between the bid and ask prices of a bond quote.

STRAIGHT BOND—any bond which is not convertible.

STREET NAME—a certificate registered in the name of a brokerage, as an owner or as the agent for a customer.

TENDER—the delivery of a certificate to the agent of a corporation.

UNDERWRITING BROKERAGE GROUP—a group of brokerages who manage the new-issue of a security.

UNDERWRITING DISCOUNT—the fee obtained by members of an underwriting brokerage group for the marketing of a new-issue, received in the form of a discount from par value of the new-issue.

Index

For Loved Ones, Friends, and Others Who Return Books Slowly—additional copies of this book may be obtained at the same outlet where this copy was purchased *or* by sending $10.00 (plus 60¢ postage) to:

California Financial Publications
3900 Shenandoah Drive
Oceanside, CA 92054